God Bless You
Veda Lee Barkley

THE PASTOR'S SOURCEBOOK

Phil. 4:13

THE PASTOR'S SOURCEBOOK

Building Blocks for Sermons

Vada Lee Barkley

Copyright © 2003 by Vada Lee Barkley.

ISBN: Softcover   1-4134-1133-9

All rights reserved. No part of this book may be reproduced or transmitted in any form or by any means, electronic or mechanical, including photocopying, recording, or by any information storage and retrieval system, without permission in writing from the copyright owner.

This book was printed in the United States of America.

To order additional copies of this book, contact:
Xlibris Corporation
1-888-795-4274
www.Xlibris.com
Orders@Xlibris.com
19215

CONTENTS

Introduction 7
Chapter 1
    Devotional Material 9
Chapter 2
    Words of Wisdom 23
Chapter 3
    Outlines 40
Chapter 4
    Sermons 64
Chapter 5
    Glimpses into Truth 110
Chapter 6
    Anecdotes 121
Chapter 7
    Thoughts on Prayer 145
Chapter 8
    Bible Lessons 155
Chapter 9
    Chuckles 166

INTRODUCTION

My late husband, Rev. Arthur E. Barkley, spent a lifetime searching the Scriptures and numerous sources pertaining to them. Like the man described in Psalms 1:3, his delight was in the "law of the Lord." And in that law he meditated day and night. He was my concordance and my commentary. The verse "O how I love thy law" on his monument describes him perfectly.

This book contains building blocks for sermons based primarily on his findings and experience.

CHAPTER 1

Devotional Material

Just Who Do You Think You Are?

There are three people in you—(1) The one your associates see (the outer person), (2) The one you see (your self-image), and (3) The one Jesus sees (the real you). Who you are then depends on whose image you focus on.

If you go by what your associates see, your chief concern will be "What do others think?" If you see only yourself, you will be discouraged and inhibited. If you see as Jesus sees, you will see what you have been, what you are, and what you can be.

If you are surrendered to God, you are cooperating with Him, enjoying His resources, doing things beyond belief, filled with divine energy and insight, and loosed from fears—poised, progressive, productive, happy, useful, and blessed. You are a blessing to others as well. Only Jesus sees what you are capable of becoming.

Nobody thought Matthew, Zacchaeus, or Martha attractive or outstanding in the least. They were all very ordinary people who seemed to be featureless personalities with no distinctive talents, social standing, nor unusual abilities, with nothing really fascinating about them.

But Jesus found them amazingly lovable. He wanted to get past mere acquaintance to really have their friendship. And the ones that were the most surprised were the lonely ones themselves.

"What can He possibly see in me?" they probably wondered

when Jesus offered His affection. Associates probably said, "What can He possibly see in them?"

Sons and daughters of God were what Jesus saw. How could He help loving them?

The World of Jesus' Day

We live in an altogether different world from that of Jesus' day. He lived where there was no continual high-pressure advertising on TV, no smoky factories, no noisy traffic of trucks and automobiles on super highways, no airplanes going through the trackless air, no skyscrapers, and no instant communications. Life was simple.

We sometimes ask, "What would Jesus do?" Would He join a labor union? To which political party would He belong? How would He react to some of our difficult situations?

People try to pigeon-hole Jesus and say He would do this or that. Our best answer is to consider the spirit of Jesus and His purpose in all His life and teaching.

He wanted life to be so that it would harmonize with God, enabling us to enjoy life abundantly and triumphantly.

When Jesus spoke, His words came from a sympathetic heart. He was frank and bold. In His utterances there was no whining, no compromise, no shifting of emphasis.

When called upon to deal with a particular situation, He dealt with it honestly.

When sympathy was needed, He gave it. When men needed rebuke, He rebuked them unsparingly.

When He faced hostile crowds, He faced them without fear.

Men like Elijah or Amos, with the Palestinian dust upon them, or Jesus of Nazareth could walk into the midst of powerful and mighty men and make them tremble like an aspen leaf. Some words of Jesus sound so harsh that we wish He hadn't spoken them.

Was the world of Jesus' day so very much different from ours? Or, in essentials, was it really different at all?

Study Josepheus' description of the Galilee that Jesus knew and loved, and to which He spoke face to face, and you find nearly all of our modern problems.

1. There was shocking over-population with all that goes with it.

    Reading the gospels, did it ever strike you how, in a moment and out of nowhere, a crowd gathers (Mark 1:33)—a crowd with so much suffering among the people, diseases in the midst that tell of poor housing and a low standard of living (Luke 9:42; 12:1)?
2. Taxes then were terrible, more drastic than ours are today—poll tax, income tax (1%), and ground tax (10% of grain).
3. There was unemployment, with many standing idle in the marketplace all day looking for a job. It all sounds familiar.

In the Sermon on the Mount, Jesus was well aware that the people He kept urging not to worry were living right on the edge. They were actually struggling, not for luxuries, but for the bare necessities of life—for food to feed their families and clothes to put on their backs.

What Is Man?

The Christian answer is that he is a restless child of earth—a child of eternity too. He is a curious mixture of dust and deity, frailty and dignity, crowned by his Creator with glory and honor, and made little less than divine.

The scientist or biologist would say that man is just a diversified arrangement of electrons, protons, and quantums. With that view we are no longer wonderfully and fearfully made in the image of God. We are only a brief incident in a long process of man over many centuries, and a very insignificant incident at that.

Surely God had some high purpose when He made the body, mind, and spirit of man. This being true, you would think that no one would ever hold himself cheaply, stoop to anything that would mar the image of God in him, or ever look with contempt on any person fashioned in God's image.

The Bible teaches that man is more than an intelligent animal or a glorified brute. It tells us that you and I have what no beast has ever had—a living soul bestowed by God Himself, a soul that will live on and on as ages upon ages roll.

Instead of saying that God created man in His own image, unbelievers tell us that our ancestors were chimpanzees and that God never made us at all. They say we started 'way back yonder when some tiny, infinitesimal speck of unexplainable grew and developed and changed—improving all along—until at last, by a series of differentiating processes, this speck was later perfected into man.

The Word tells us that God formed us for His pleasure. He meant for us to see Him, live with Him, and draw our life and sustenance from Him. Unfortunately, we have been guilty of that "foul revolt" of which Milton speaks when describing the rebellion of Satan and his hosts.

The whole work of God in redemption is to undo the tragic effects of that foul revolt and to bring us back into right and eternal relationship with Him.

When our restless hearts feel a yearning for God and we say, "I will arise and go to my Father," that is the first step. And the "journey of a thousand miles begins with a first step."

Mary and Martha
Luke 10: 38-42

Mary sat at Jesus' feet and listened to every pearl that dropped from His lips. It wasn't every day that one could hear the Master, and she didn't want to miss this opportunity.

Martha was the type who would hoe weeds; Mary was the type who would smell the flowers.

Here was the Messiah, the Savior, God Incarnate, not the kind of person to whom one gives orders. But Martha lost sight of who it was with whom she was dealing. She should have been sitting at His feet, listening to Him, but she was challenging Him instead. She attempted to minister to Jesus when she desperately needed to be ministered to by Him.

> It is written, "He that hath seen me hath seen the father."
> John 14:9

I can never accuse God of being hard with penitent sinners, for Jesus wrote the record of a sinner in the sand and scratched it out.

I can never accuse God of being unmindful of my humble state, for Jesus took a towel and washed His disciples' feet.

I can never accuse God of favoring the rich at the neglect of the poor, for when Jesus set up His hall of fame, He put on its chief pedestal a poor widow with two mites in her hand.

I can never accuse God of being careless or unmindful of common people, for Jesus went to dine with publicans and sinners.

I know that God does not forget His own, because Jesus showed me a father standing at the crossroads, shading his eyes, watching for a wandering boy to come home. And when that boy came, the father saw to it that the feast was made ready, that there was a robe to replace the rags, and that the feast did not begin until the prodigal was in his place at the table.

The Christian Offer

Jesus offers us nothing less than a new kind of life. It is a share in the life of God.

God offers His power for our frustration. Some people spend the greater part of their lives putting limitations on the power of

God. But, with God, all things are possible. The word "impossible" has no place in the vocabulary of a Christian.

God offers His serenity for our chaos, His truth for our uncertainty, His goodness for our moral failure, and His joy for our sorrow. Most important of all, He offers us His love.

1. The Christian life is daily loving Christ more and understanding Him better. What God has in store for us is a life in which we are on the right terms with God, with ourselves, and with our fellowman.
2. The Christian life is a life in which we can cope with the great moments and also with the everyday duties.
3. The Christian life is a life in which Jesus Christ lives again.
4. The Christian life offers to us here and now a quality of life which we have not known before. When Christ enters our lives, we really begin to live.

Before Jesus came, God was a distant stranger whom only a very few might approach, and that at the peril of their lives. But, because of what Jesus was and what He did, God has become the friend of every man.

Once people thought of Him as One to be feared and dreaded. Now we see Him as a loving Father who invites all who will to come to Him.

However wonderful life on earth with Christ may be, we know that the best is yet to come.

So we know the wonder of past sins forgiven, the thrill of this present life lived with Jesus, and the hope of the greater life which is yet to be.

The Kind of Gospel I want

I want a gospel that has length and breadth and depth. I want it to have content, to be full.

I want miracles in my religion. I want a religion that can

subdue kingdoms, stop the mouths of lions, escape the edge of the sword, make weak men strong, put to flight the armies of aliens.

I want God to do for me what no one on earth can do. I want my Lord to be holy and righteous, having justice tempered with love, and to so love the world that anyone, anywhere who would believe would not perish.

I want to see Him as our forefathers did in a thousand campfires, so that with His help I will not be afraid.

I want my Eternal City to have foundations, with God as Architect and Builder, and to know that in that home all His children will meet at last.

The Mystery of Jesus

This man, Jesus, was an historical character. He was a member of our human family. And He lived His life here upon earth. If we were to attempt to deal with all His sayings, we would find many of them hard to understand. If we were to attempt to grapple with His personality, we would find ourselves face to face with mysteries too deep to be fathomed.

His disciples did not begin with the mystery of His person, nor with His sayings, which were too hard for them to understand. They began by getting near Him, looking at him with their own eyes, and listening to Him with their own ears.

To be a Christian is to admire Jesus sincerely and devotedly. We have reached the conclusion for ourselves that He was right and that no one else was so right.

Now that we have tried our chaos of cults, we find that there is none like Him. He stood against the Roman world. We can be assured that He can stand against ours. And He will still be standing when our great civilization has gone the way of the scrap heap.

The fundamental difficulty with our civilization is that it has never made up its mind as to what life is all about. Only Jesus can give us the answer.

We must recognize His humanity. He was a real man. He had every appearance of a man. He came into the world as other children do, but His birth is a mystery. The doctrine of the virgin birth need not stagger us, however, because we are totally unable to unravel the mystery of our own birth.

He was not only a man, but He was God as well. The Scriptures tell us that Jesus Christ is God. Three times in John's gospel the Jews tried to kill Him, in each case, because He claimed deity. Christ is called "Lord" and "the First and the Last," and He accepted those titles.

Jesus claimed pre-existence (John 8:58; 17:24; 11:25). He was present at the creation of all things (John 1:3). Wherever His people meet today, He is there.

He claimed omniscience and omnipotence. He knew about His death and foretold it before it happened. He claimed the power to forgive sins. He showed His power over nature, demons, disease, even life and death.

Some look upon Him as an accident, but the sinfulness of man and the holiness of God made Calvary a necessity.

His death was propitiation, a substitution, a ransom. His resurrection was the ultimate proof of His divinity.

Easter

Like some vast mountain, some mighty Everest, Jesus Christ dominates the landscape of human life and human history. Compared to Him, all others seem puny and insignificant. The great names of history have faded into oblivion. Yet this peasant—this strangely gifted Preacher and Teacher—is the greatest Man who ever lived and who still lives today. He has charmed the human race for more than twenty centuries.

On Easter Sunday we remind ourselves that this mighty Conqueror has charged the citadel of Satan, made conquest of Death, and robbed the grave of its victory forever.

Angels had announced His birth at Bethlehem. Now they announce His resurrection, the birth of new hope for the world.

It was appropriate that Jesus should rise from the dead while it was yet dark. For He who is the light of the world had come to dispel its darkness.

It is appropriate that Easter should be celebrated with song. For no doubt the angels in Heaven who sang at Jesus' birth burst into a song of victory at the resurrection from the tomb in Joseph's garden.

It is appropriate that Easter be celebrated with flowers. For He who arose is the Lily of the Valley and the Rose of Sharon.

Like flowers springing forth to beautify the earth at this season, the bodies of His deceased saints shall come forth on the resurrection morning, clothed in the beauty of immortality. For when God's angel rolled away the stone from the door of the tomb and sat upon it, he gave assurance that it should remain open never again to be closed.

If the truth of the risen Lord could have been destroyed, it would have been silenced long before now. For more than twenty centuries men have worked at that impossible task. They have failed. Jesus Christ is alive!

God's Love

Savanarola, Knox, and Luther said that men were not worth the trouble they had given God to save them. Naught but love—matchless, mighty, limitless love—could or would have led Jesus to the cross for our sins.

Where is a man to find words to describe such love? Human language is beggared, human minds confounded, and human hearts limited when faced with the overpowering expression of the love of God in the dripping wounds of the crucified.

In these trying, troubled, distraught, disheartening, disappointing days, we need the proof of that love which the cross offers.

There it is, written in the giant letters of Christ's death, written in unmistakable terms across the pages of God's dealing with men, written in the blessed words of the gospel. "For God so loved the world . . ."

The Children of God
I John 3

John begins by reminding us that we should remember our privileges. To his readers he said that it was their privilege to be called the sons of God. We *are* the children of God.

The New Testament speaks many times of adoption. Jesus speaks of a new birth as well.

While all men are children of God in that we owe our lives to Him, we become children of God, in the intimate and loving sense of the word, only by an act of God's grace and the response of our hearts.

John said that the Christian is on the way to seeing God and to being like Him.

No Christian can make sin the policy of his life. Obviously, when John wrote this third chapter, he preached against a sinning religion. He wrote: "He that commiteth sin is of the devil; for the devil sinneth from the beginning" (v.8a). In addition, he wrote: "Whosoever abideth in him sinneth not: Whosoever sinneth hath not seen him, neither known him" (v.6). "Whosoever is born of God doth not commit sin, because his seed remains in him; and he cannot sin, because he is born of God" (v.9). My little children, these things write I unto you that ye sin not. And *if* {not when} any man sin, we have an advocate with the Father, Jesus Christ the righteous" (2:1). Ezekiel quotes the Lord as saying, "The soul that sinneth, it shall die" (18:20).

Evidently Paul had never heard of the doctrine of eternal security—once a son, always a son—for he wrote: "But I keep under my body, and bring it unto subjection: lest that by any means, when I have preached to others, I myself should be a castaway" (I Cor. 9:27). If that doctrine were as important as some believe, surely God would have included it in the Theology 101 course He taught Paul in the Arabian Desert.

Jesus Himself didn't seem to know about it. He said to the woman taken in adultery, "Neither do I condemn thee: go, and sin no more" (John 8:11). Was He making an impossible demand of her? Or did He expect her to commit suicide? Is it possible that our God who hates sin has so created us that we can resist Him, yet we cannot resist the devil?

The human situation is full of things that try to take our faith away. But Jesus promised that the Holy Spirit would give us power to overcome temptation.

If God cannot deliver His children from sin, Christ failed in His mission to "destroy the works of the devil" (v.8).

The world did its worst to Jesus. It did everything humanly possible to break Him and to eliminate Him. And it failed. We wonder why God should create a world which would bring Him nothing but trouble. But John assures us that the child of God is emancipated from the power of the devil.

As a child of God, the Christian is on the side of God against the world. He is conscious that he has entered into that reality which is God. That relationship enables him to conquer the world, the flesh, and the devil.

The Essence of Christianity

In its very essence, Christianity is a religion committed to making a difference in the world. We sense an anti-Christian spirit abroad in our age. It's the same as that which caused our first parents to fall. It is merely wearing a new dress.

People today do not necessarily dismiss Jesus as a mythical figure or deny that He said some really fine things or did good deeds. Most do not reject Him outright as the hope of the world. They spurn His spirit because they refuse to follow His teachings. Perhaps in some distant future—at least before they die—but not now!

We teach our youth high ideals and standards of conduct. When they leave home with high hopes of practicing that lifestyle, however, they are ridiculed by so-called wiser and more experienced people.

Politicians, businessmen, professors, and other influential figures often sneer at such standards. To fit in with the grown-up, sophisticated world, our youth must compromise their convictions. In its opposition to Jesus and His teachings, the world is subtle, yet effective.

The god of Mammon has a strange way of putting down the finest, highest, and best in people.

Our god of Fashion says: "Everybody's doing it. You can't afford to be out of style."

The god of Tradition keeps us in a rut, preventing justice and mercy from flowing as a river.

These gods and scores of others constantly threaten all of us who follow Christ. But, at the risk of being ostracized and considered "odd balls," we who profess His name are committed to making a difference in our world. That is the essence of Christianity.

The Reality of Jesus

Too many of us are not really convinced of the reality of Jesus. We want to think of Him as a teacher who said many nice things which are pleasant to repeat. We don't want to be like the boy from Eastern Europe who was being tried for his refusal to bear arms.

He was brought before the judge, and he carefully gave his reasons, showing that he had thought it all out very clearly and had a reason for his opinions.

The judge listened to the end, and then he said in a rather impatient manner: "Young man, your position would be logical if the Kingdom of God had come; but it hasn't."

The boy replied, "It has for me."

Counting the Cost

John Bunyan tells the story of a man with "a stout countenance" looking boldly at what the difficulties of the spiritual life were.

He said, "Set down my name, Sire, for I have looked at this one thing—looked it in the face, and, cost what it may, I mean to have Christlikeness and I will!"

This is the first definite step towards making religion real.

Love vs. Law

A distraught couple appeared in domestic court in New York. They had been married ten years, and they were having marital trouble.

They had problems trying to explain their situation to their lawyers. Both were trying to see how little they could yield in order to get by or to save face.

I've tried to contrast their spirit and attitude in the court room with what must have been their attitude during courtship, when each was trying to see how much could be done to please the other.

When we are merely keeping a law, we try to see how little we can do; but with love, we try to see how much we can do to please the other.

That's true, not only in human relationships, but it is also true in our relationship with Christ.

Keeping in Tune with God

The late George Stewart said, "I was at a home one time where a string ensemble was playing the most beautiful dinner music.

"While the musicians were eating, the children tampered with the strings. When the musicians took up their instruments again to play, there was a horrible discord.

"The key note was struck and all the instruments were tuned again, and the music was sweet once more.

"And there was a time once in the Garden of Eden when man loved God and there was music everywhere, but Satan brought a discord, and it has filled the world ever since. But, at Calvary, Jesus Christ struck the key note, 'Love one another as I have loved you,' and the world is full of music now when men's hearts are full of love."

Unfortunately, however, not everyone's heart is in tune.

The Master Teacher

Jesus' words seem yet to echo in the air. The passing of centuries has not hushed His voice. None of His words have lost any of their power.

How could they fail when no man ever spoke as He spoke?

The greatest Teacher of all the ages speaks. He speaks of the kingdom of God. He shows us that it is not a structure to be built; it is not a thesis to be defended; it is instead a life to be developed.

Some men spend the greater part of their lives putting limitations on the power of God. But with Him all things are possible. The word *impossible* has no place in the vocabulary of a Christian.

There was always something daring about Jesus. He loved to fling down a challenge before impossible situations.

CHAPTER 2

Words of Wisdom

Wouldn't you think that Jesus, with only three years to go, would have visited Rome and Athens and sought out all available publicity, called on celebrities, appeared at forums and symposiums in an effort to get His message across?

Our moderns would have rushed from dawn to midnight, making every minute count, held public debates, and put on healing services everywhere possible.

Instead Jesus stayed in an obscure little Roman province, talked with few folks, comparatively speaking. He mingled with ordinary people. He exasperated his brothers by not performing in Jerusalem and using His unique power to get the right things done.

It is all foreign to our American way of doing things. Our Lord would have been the despair of any modern publicity agent. The first thirty years of His life are hidden in almost complete silence.

Often when He performed a miracle He requested that it not be publicized. The Transfiguration was not revealed to a crowd, and the Last Supper was hidden from the public.

What about the greatest event of all, the resurrection? That would have been the greatest extravaganza of all time! Why didn't Jesus appear before Herod and Caiaphas and Pontius Pilate and preach in Jerusalem? It would have accomplished in an instant what we have tried for centuries to prove, and the world doesn't believe yet!

Nobody but believers saw Him. The greatest secret of all

time has been confided to us. Yet it is not a secret to be hidden, but a story to be told.

He is above all Someone to present. For He is the Resurrection and the Life!

The Truce of God

Whittier has a verse in which he speaks of those special moments of grace which God gives to the soul. He calls them the "truce of God."

By the truce of God, I mean a special appeal to turn away from sin and to choose God and righteousness.

Peter had such a moment when he denied his Master in the courtyard of the high priest and Jesus turned and looked at him.

Judas had such a moment, when Jesus washed his feet at the Last Supper and later said to him, "That thou doest, do quickly."

Pilate had a truce of God granted to him when he confronted Jesus. His wife wrote a letter to him urging him to have nothing to do with "this just man." To his credit, he tried to release Jesus. But the political risk was too great. He turned Christ over to the mob to be scourged and crucified. Then Pilate washed his hands.

Miscellaneous Remarks

If we find ourselves lost amid the traditions and theories of religion, we can always go back to Jesus and the gospels and find truth that is so clear and understandable that we wonder why we have ever felt it necessary to go beyond it.

Jesus really gave only one commandment, "Follow me!" He never meant it to be intellectually difficult to begin the Christian life.

We do not need to know about Him so much as we need to know Him.

I shall never cease to be amazed that so many people have never thought their way through to any well defined views concerning Jesus Christ.

They have no overmastering convictions about Who He was and is; what He is doing; and what He has done.

Such people are merely existing. They have never known what it means to really live. They remind me of the Roman soldiers who took Jesus out and nailed Him to the cross. When they had finished that gruesome task, they lifted the cross and dropped it into its place.

Then they fell to their knees and started gambling for His clothing. So far as we know they never looked up again. Hanging just above their heads was the Son of God, Savior of the world, the hope of the human race, and our hope for time and eternity. But they were so engrossed in the pursuit of their own interests that never once did they look up to see Him.

Many people are like that. They don't know that His was a unique life, lived out upon the earth among men in order that it might be lived over in you and me.

Christianity is not a thing to be argued about. It is a life to be lived, and, therefore, something to be experienced.

One evening a group met for Bible study and sharing.
"Now it's time to exchange Christmas gifts," said the leader.
Silence followed. No one was prepared for that.
"How about giving each other gifts that cannot be bought at a store?" the leader suggested.
After a few minutes, answers came pouring in.
One man said, "This year my wife and I are going to give each other a weekend of our uninterrupted time."
Another said, "We promise to pray for every person in the group for the next month."

A wife said, "I promise to give my husband the gift of self-respect."

Isn't that what giving is all about?

The distressing thing about our present situation is the great number of people who have said "yes" to Christianity intellectually and have stopped there.

This is not an easy day to live for Christ, but has any day ever been easy?

Life seems to be forever confronting us with unusual situations, difficulties, problems, and perplexities, then wanting to know what we plan to do about them.

In the Bible God gives us revelations of Himself which lead us to worship, promises of salvation which stimulate our faith, and commandments which demand our obedience.

A vast number of people who flock to the cults and heresies of our day go in the vain hope that peace of mind can be attained without profound spiritual alterations.

No people can long endure without an ultimate standard. Even the most primitive tribe is wise enough to teach its children that there is a final loyalty.

We have accepted the double standard with a vengeance. It is wrong if *you* do it, but all right if *I* do it. It is wrong today, but it will be right tomorrow. It was wrong under those circumstances, but it is right under these circumstances. We desperately need some strong voices to set some standards.

Great as the universe has proved itself to be, man has proved himself to be greater.

Men have said that the one thing which gives them hope for justice is a future life long enough, exact enough, and wise enough to settle questions which were unsettled here.

It is the man who is living a life broad enough and good enough to last forever who expects that it will. The nearer a person lives to God, the surer he is of being with Him both here and hereafter.

An Arab philosopher was asked how he knew God.
He answered, "How do I know whether a man or a camel has passed my tent during the night? By the footprints, of course."
We do not see God; we see only His footprints as He goes past our tent of flesh.
If we can find near our tent of flesh the signs of His coming, they will serve us better than argument.

The Eternal God in the person of His Son got off the throne of the universe, came down into a wicked world, was born in a stable, cradled in a manger, grew up in poverty, lived amid hardship, and had no place to lay His head.
He welcomed sinners, submitted to the judgment of men, and gave His life for the whole world of lost people.

Just when we think we have found a formula to fit the facts of life something unpredictable turns up and makes our neat, ship-shaped logic look absurd.
Just when we think we have established the rule, we discover a host of exceptions that play havoc with the axioms which we thought were water-tight and secure.

Only God can open the gate of the Kingdom of Heaven; for thousands of people Christ has opened it.

Only God can break the chains of a man's sinful nature; for thousands Christ has broken them.

Many have come to think that God's ways with us must always be involved, His truths deep and hard to understand, and our experiences with Him strange and mystifying.

No doubt we often miss His message to us in some simple events in life because we think of His coming to us only in some rare, momentous events.

God's voice is really a very personal and intimate one. The best time to hear Him speak to us is in our times of trouble and pain.

An infidel once said, "If I could be sure of a hereafter and know that I would meet the loved ones gone before, I would crawl on my hands and knees from Boston to San Francisco just to gain that knowledge." He wouldn't have to crawl at all if he would honestly get on his knees before God and ask Him to take control of his life.

It is actually just as difficult to *not* believe in God as it is to believe. Sit down sometime and try to prove to yourself that there is no God, and see the impasses you confront.

1. You'll have to say that the world was created by accident.
2. You'll have to say that this marvelous mind of man, which can create wonders, which has invented so many things for your comfort and happiness, came by accident.
3. You'll have to say that this soul, which loves and inspires

us to higher heights, is in no wise connected to a power that makes for righteousness in the world.
4. You'll have to say it has all come together by accident, that God has no part in the affairs of this world.
5. You'll have to say that God does not answer prayer.

Does the existence of God make any difference in your life? The biggest heresy of our age is that of admitting God's existence but denying His relevance. According to a Gallup poll, 97 percent of Americans believe in God. Unfortunately, no one could say that God plays a significant role in the lives of 97 out of 100 Americans.

The great comfort of knowing and serving the Lord Jesus Christ is a strong, wonderful experience.

It is like wind to a boat, with sails up, sitting in a great calm, going nowhere.

It is like the gift of a job to a man who has been desperately seeking a job for a long time.

It is like a pitcher of ice water to a dehydrated body.

It is like a sumptuous meal to a starving man.

It is like the restoration of health to a terminally ill patient.

Jesus and His way of life are not a burden, unless He is the kind of burden that wings are to a bird. Isn't it a shame that the little bird has to have wings attached to its little body? Yet those burdens called wings give the bird power to soar, to fly, and to live.

Most common conceptions of the earthly environment of Jesus put Him in a remote country, far removed from the forces which shape a civilization. But such a conception cannot stand. The lines of civilization were shifting westward before the time of Jesus, but Palestine was an important location. It was the place where East and West met and mingled. Rome might rule the world, but, to the Jew, Jerusalem was a place apart.

A person might live in ease and luxury and on the fat of the land. He might have the finest kind of house and biggest bank account and yet not have peace.

On the other hand, one might be starving for food, languishing in prison, or living a life devoid of all comforts and yet be at perfect peace.

The only source of peace is doing the will of God.

Did anyone watching Jesus in those Galilean days ever see Him irritated? Think of what He had to put up with, sharing everyone's hurts, all their sins and sorrows, feeling them as personally as though they were His own.

Utterly amazed at Jesus' composure under all the false accusations, indignities, and torture heaped upon Him, Pilate said, "Behold the man!" or "What a man!"

Notice Jesus' words when He was preparing His followers for His going away: "Peace I leave with you, my peace I give unto you . . . ." John 14:27). Note the words "*my peace.*"

Without God we are absolutely hopeless, helpless, and undone. The ungodly elements of this age are set for our destruction. The natural man is beset by a thousand enemies of righteousness. The easy-going moral standards of our day have fallen to an all-time low. But God has promised great blessings to everyone who will serve Him wholeheartedly.

The destiny of the American nation depends upon the kind of homes we are making for our children.

Delinquent children are usually the products of delinquent parents. We cannot live in a family with children without teaching them for or against God's way.

A child knows when his father is putting God first and when he is not.

As Christians we are not called to be conformed to the world, but to be transformed. We are called to live a separate and distinct life according to the teachings of Jesus and to proclaim a vital, life-saving message, especially to our children.

From all eternity God has loved you with an everlasting love. Patiently He has been working with you, trying to fashion something beautiful of your life. He made you a great person high on the scale of excellence: able to look before, after, and up towards Him; able to think His vast thoughts after Him; and able to hold communion with Him.

As your example, He sent Jesus Christ, in Whose life you have learned what your life should be, and at Whose hands you have received grace to help in every time of need. He has set before you great and precious promises and assured you that they are not mere dreams that pass away.

How does faith in God help us today?

Why is Christ the most unusual and wonderful figure in history? Because He was so certain that God is here among us; that He is alive and concerned about us; that if we call, He will answer; that even if we forget Him, He remembers us and helps us; that we are never alone, but the Father is always with us.

Then trouble comes. "How can I bear it?" your heart cries.

You can't. But you don't have to; you don't face it in your own strength. In the most trying circumstances, "Closer is He than breathing, nearer than hands and feet." Since you can draw upon all His resources, you can bear the unbearable.

Ernest Scott says, "The knowledge that the world with all its dangers and accidents is overruled by God enables us to trust God even in the dark."

If you know Christ—if He has been the strength to your weakness, comfort to your sorrow, and light to your dark way in hours when flesh and spirit fail you; if He, the Son of

Righteousness, has risen upon you with healing in His wings—then you hold in your possession that for which this world, in its pathetic plight, is waiting and hoping.

A group of ministers, educators, and civic leaders were talking about Jesus.

One educator said, "I guess we can't always follow Jesus in everything, for, of course, He was sometimes wrong."

A minister said, "Did you say that we could not always follow Jesus in everything?"

"Yes, I did," replied the other.

"That being the case, my friend, whom would you recommend?" Peter asked that question long ago, "Lord, to whom shall we go?"

"What would you do if in the next few minutes Christ should suddenly appear before you?" That was the question asked one evening of Charles Lamb, the British essayist.

Literary friends visiting him were wondering what their reaction would be if some of the outstanding figures of the past should enter the room.

"Suppose Dante should knock at our door," one suggested, "how enthusiastically we would rise to get to shake his hand whose poetry so glowingly describes the beauty of Paradise!"

"What if Shakespeare were to come?"

Lamb's face brightened, "How I would fling my arms up to welcome that king of thoughtful men!"

After a short pause there was another question: "Suppose Christ should enter this place?"

Instantly, with a voice of deepest reverence, Lamb replied, "We would all fall on our knees before Him, of course, and kiss the hem of His garment."

It is hard to understand the fact of suffering when people tell us that God is love.

If a stranger from another far-off planet should drop suddenly into this world, he would see hospitals full of patients with various diseases, prisons crowded with evil men and seducers, and homes filled with sadness and crying. He would see fields of battle strewn with the dead bodies of the fallen.

Nations would be languishing under tyranny and people starving from famine. In addition to these troubles, they would be enduring the devastation from floods and hurricanes.

But God is with us in our troubles and that means victory.

If your soul is stumbling through the gloom, reach out for the hand of God!

A British writer tells about spending some time on a farm during World War II.

The farmer and his wife, John and Mary, were genuine Christians, with the joy of the Lord in their hearts.

He said that a girl came to work on the farm during the summer months. She was a very modern type, who had no use whatsoever for religion.

As she watched John and Mary, however, she began to see that there must be something to being a Christian.

When this writer was leaving, she said to him, "I know there is something to Christianity. I try to read the Bible, but I find it difficult. I try to pray, but I don't know the right words. But I'm not worrying; I'm sure I will find God by following Mary."

I have read that when a man wishes to become a member of the Benedictine order of monks, he is accepted for a year on probation.

During that year his clothes which he wore in the world hang in his cell. At any time he can take off his monk's habit, put on his worldly clothes, and walk out. No one will think the worse of him.

Only at the end of the year are his clothes taken away. It is with open eyes and a full knowledge of what he is doing that he enters this religious order.

So it is with Christianity, Jesus does not want followers who have not stopped to count the cost.

There is something better than having joy at the thought of victory over death.

In Northern Ireland, a peddler called at a certain house.

The householder said, "It's a grand thing to be saved!"

The peddler replied, "Yes, but I know something better!"

In astonishment the householder asked, "What could possibly be better?"

The answer? "The companionship with the Risen Christ. That is even better than salvation; to know that I am saved, that I have eternal life, that I'm not going to hell, yes, that is wonderful. But the companionship of the Risen Christ is more wonderful!"

God saved us not only to take us to heaven, but also to give us fellowship with Him. He is more interested in us than we are in Him. He wants our companionship. He wants us close to Him.

He wants to duplicate Himself in us. Christianity is actually a duplication of Jesus Christ in us.

How can God reveal Christ in us? God wants us to be conformed to the image of His Son wherever we are: in work, in leisure, in every place and in every situation.

My prayer is, "Lord, keep chiseling on me and working with me until someone recognizes that I am living in Christ."

I once read about a visit that the Shah of Persia, an ancestor of Shah Mohammed Palavi, made to the United Kingdom. While in London, he was taken to hear a great orchestra which was to play Beethoven's Ninth Symphony.

All the instruments were being tuned before the symphony

began. Each musician was testing the violin strings or his flute or other horn. While all this tuning was taking place, the Shah sat enraptured.

His companions and translators found to their dismay that all through this testing, the Shah thought he was listening to the symphony. They had difficulty making him believe that it had not really begun.

It is likely that many people today, hearing the miscellaneous noises of religious controversies, get the idea that they are listening to the meaning of the religion of Jesus Christ. But Christianity is far greater and far more harmonious than anything like that.

Vance Havener says that one big danger that we Christians face today is the fed-up spirit.

"If we believers do not somehow manage to become humble and child-like and receptive, and rejoice and weep together in our meeting instead of sitting like a bunch of stenographers collecting material for our notebooks, we are going to turn out to be the driest generation of saints in all church history."

There was once a farmer who lived on a small farm all his life, grew tired of it, and wanted to sell it. He decided to sell the old place and buy another one more to his liking. So he listed the farm with a realtor. And this realtor started writing an advertisement for the paper and trade journals.

Before giving it to the newspaper, he read it over to the farmer. It was a glowing description of the property. He told of its ideal location, nice buildings, fertile acres, and well bred stock.

"Wait a minute," said the farmer. "Read that again, and read it slow!"

The realtor read it again.

The farmer said, "You know, I've changed my mind. I'm not

going to sell. All my life I've been looking for a place like that."

In one of his books, Clovis Chappell tells of a liquor store in Chicago which had a sign over the door "God bless America."

What blasphemy! What the boozer is saying to God is this: "You bless America while I help to send it to hell!"

God can bless America only as we walk with Him in His wonderful way.

In his book *If God Cares, Why Do I Still Have Problems?* Dr. Lloyd Ogilvie tells the following story:

A boy at odds with his family went away from home. When he heard that his father had died, he came for the funeral but didn't sit with the family.

After the funeral he went back to the city, where he lived in poverty, unaware that his father had remembered him in his will. The boy was rich beyond his fondest dreams; yet he was living in poverty.

One dad said to another, "I'm not a model father. All I'm trying to do is to so live that when people tell my son that he reminds them of me, he'll stick out his chest instead of his tongue."

The late Rev. Dick Shepherd of St. Martins-in-the Fields, London, said that being a Christian consists not only in refraining from doing things which no gentleman would do anyway, but in doing good things which a mere gentleman might not think to do.

After a man has climbed so high, his friends quit wondering how much higher he'll go, so they start shaking the ladder.

John Henry Newman has a remarkable passage in which he imagines what it would be like to look out into the world and see no trace of God. "That would be," he says, "Just as if I were to look into a mirror and not see my face."

Think of looking into a mirror and seeing only a blank.

The story goes that St. Bernard told his monks that however early they might wake and rise for prayer in their chapel on a cold midwinter morning, a fine summer morn, or even in the dead of night, they would always find God awake before them, waiting for them; that it was God Who had awakened them to seek His face.

Because I cannot hide what is in me, and because when God sees what is in me, He still loves me, I'm able at last to take my great need to His exceeding great love.

A traveler to Africa was watching a nun who was also a nurse dressing the raw sores of a leper. The sores were revolting, gruesome, and repulsive.

As the traveler watched her, not getting any closer than necessary, he said, "I wouldn't do that for ten thousand dollars!"

Without bothering to look up, the nurse said, "Neither would I."

When Adlai Stevenson was running for governor of Illinois, he was told by one of his supporters that he would certainly have the vote of every thinking person in the state.

"Trouble is," replied Stevenson, "I'll need to have a majority!"

In that strange book *Sartor Resartus,* there is a description of Carlyle's philosopher gazing out from his high attic window across the city at midnight, musing on the age-old mysteries of life and death, love and suffering, hope and misery.

Down below, the dark streets stretch away for miles, with half a million people all crammed together—the joyful and the sad, men dying and children being born, some praying, others weeping.

"All these" he says," are heaped and huddled together with only a little carpentry and masonry between them, a kind of microcosm of humanity gathered there beneath the covering of the vast, indifferent night.

"But," he says, "I sit above it all. I am alone with the stars."

Is God like that? From Rachael weeping for her children to Jesus suffering on His cross, to every troubled person in our world today, there rises the question "Why?"

"Why should this happen? Why should these troubles come?"

With so many forms of trouble in this world—physical, mental, emotional, and spiritual—it is hard to explain why if God is love He permits so much suffering in the world. A lot of the tragedies could be due to the fact that there are certain uniform principles which govern our universe. When we break those laws—intentionally or otherwise—we suffer the consequences.

From the inner reaches of New York harbor, out through the narrows where deep water begins, stretches Ambrose Channel, 16 miles long.

It is not very wide, however, and in the old days it was very difficult to navigate that distance through a storm or in heavy fog.

Then engineers laid a cable up the center of the channel. That cable carries alternating electric signals which are picked up by the ships as they pass into or out of the harbor.

The strength of these signals tells the pilot when he is directly above the cable or when he is "on the beam." In that way ships can move into and out of the harbor safely. No matter how black the night or how heavy the fog, progress is possible.

For the Christian there is a still, small voice which we can hear and we need never lose our way.

We see how God works in history from the story of Oliver Cromwell and John Hampden, two stalwart makers of England.

In the days when they were still almost unknown, they were impatient with the way the king and the court and the government were ruining the nation and bringing it down to disaster. They decided that the only course for them was to leave the country and never set foot in it again.

They had heard about the new colony beyond the ocean where the winds of freedom blew and life was clean.

News came to them that a ship would soon be making the Atlantic crossing. Quietly they took their places on board. Everything was in readiness for the voyage, when, at the last minute, messengers dashed in with orders from the king that on no account were they to be allowed to sail.

Frustrated and angry at this turn of events, Cromwell and Hampden came ashore. It was the ruin of their dream, but it was that ruin which gave Cromwell to England and shaped the course of history.

When Prof. M.A. Linebarger came back from the Far East, he said, "Americans believe in spiritual things but they try to buy them by material means—by dollars, by gifts, by aid.

"Communists believe in material things, but they offer people something to join, something to do, and something to fight for." Can it be that the Christian faith retreats before its enemies, who are making their appeal on a call to action while the church offers people something very pale and anemic, static, and relatively harmless?

CHAPTER 3

Outlines

Pentecost

I. It was a day in history.
II. It was and is an event in human experience.
III. It was and is designed by God.
IV. It met and meets His requirements.
V. It launched the greatest rescue effort in history.
VI. It will be gloriously culminated in the Rapture.

Time to Seek the Lord

"It is time to seek the Lord"
Hosea 10:12

I. It is time to seek the Lord because of the person against whom you have sinned.
II. It is time to seek the Lord because of the hardening tendency of sin.
III. It is time to seek the Lord because of your influence over others.
IV. It is time to seek the Lord because the moments are passing so swiftly.
V. It is time to seek the Lord because of the passing opportunities.
VI. It is time to seek the Lord because your soul may be lost.

A. There's no death in hell,
B. There is no love in hell,
C. There is no light in hell,
D. There is no hope in hell.

Eternity will never be spent.
We hold our eternal destiny in our own power. We can go to heaven if we chose. But it is time to seek the Lord.

The Parable of the Soils
Luke 8:5-8

I. The closed mind—wayside hearers, open for everything
II. The shallow mind—no really deep thoughts
III. The pre-occupied mind—torn by different loyalties
IV. The open mind—ready to hear and to act

The Picture Gallery

To read the parables of Jesus is to move through a wonderful picture gallery—the sower, the prodigal son, and others. It is a gallery filled with the most wonderful and fascinating portraits, including Jesus' self-portrait.

I. A picture of the marvelous patience of God
II. How evil tends to grow
III. God is bewildered—"What shall I do?"
IV. The futile attempt of man to run away from God or to silence God

A Prescription for Spiritual and Mental Health

I. A committed life (Josh. 24:14; Rom. 12:1)
II. A joyous spirit (Pro. 17:22; Phil. 4:4)
III. A grateful heart (Eph. 5:19)
IV. A clean mind (Phil 4:8)

V. A clear conscience (Acts 24:16)
VI. A forgiving spirit
VII. A willingness to be used of God

It is not so much our ability that counts as our pliability in the hands of God.

"Wrinkles" that Hurt Our Holiness
Eph. 5:27

1. A failure to return borrowed articles
2. Slackness in keeping the Lord's Day
3. Slackness in honoring God's house
4. A slovenly personal appearance
5. Failure to keep our promises
6. Living beyond our means—going in debt to buy things we don't need to impress people we don't like, trying to keep up with the Joneses
7. Speaking evil of others
8. Failure to discipline our children
9. Unwillingness to carry our share of the financial load of the church
10. Lack of good manners—rudeness when driving a car; disregard for the feelings of others; forgetting good manners at home or church

The Church at Antioch

1. The church had a strong corporate sense.
2. This corporate sense included material things.
3. It was a church without race or class.
4. It held in its fellowship a blend of the radical and the conservative.
5. It held together strong men who differed on principles and persons.

6. It was redemptive.
7. It was also creative. Paul and Barnabas were set apart.

The Christian Religion in Essence

1. It is not a philosophy of life. We need more than a philosophy to hold us steady in the storms of life.
2. It is not a moral code. Of course it will provide you with that—the most sublime code ever. But men are not set afire by a moral code.
3. It is not a social creed. Christ has been behind more social reforms than any other leader who ever lived. But no amount of social passion can work the miracle of regeneration.
4. It is a personal relationship with the purest One who ever walked this earth.

The power of Jesus is unlimited; His power is available. Thousands can testify that Jesus helped when earthly supports failed, that He cured when medical science offered no hope, and that He supplied their need when money was gone.

To Please God and Be Saved

1. We must believe in God—Eternal, Almighty, unchanging.
2. We must believe that Jesus Christ is God's Son and our Savior.
3. We must believe in the Holy Spirit, our Enabler.
4. We must believe in miracles—the greatest of which is that of a changed life.
5. We must believe in angels.
6. We must believe in the devil and evil spirits.
7. We must believe that there is to be a Judgment Day.
8. We must believe in heaven.
9. We must believe in a literal hell for all those who disobey and fight against God.

The Rich Young Man
Mark 10:22

1. He came at the right time.
2. He came in the right spirit.
3. He came for the right purpose.
4. He came to the right place.

This story may sound old to some, but it is not old; it happens every day.

1. This young man had assets: moral standing, wealth, prestige, religion, social standing.
2. Assets Jesus offered him: a Savior, a new concept of the cross, treasures in heaven.
3. Mistakes he made:

    a. He had a shallow idea of goodness.
    b. He had a false concept of religion.
    c. He was willing to give Jesus any place in his life except first place.
    d. He lacked eternal life.
    e. He went away sorrowful.

When Things Go Wrong for You

Some people are more afraid to live than to die; that's why they take their own lives. If you just knew it, probably everyone you meet is waging a real, desperate battle. When things go wrong, let's remember

1. Things are not always what they seem to be.
2. Things are not as bad as we may at the moment suppose. Very few things are going to turn out as you think they will. If you don't believe that, just keep a diary and check it later.

If there aren't any dangers or problems around us at the time, we manufacture a few, or failing there, we're simply bored stiff.
3. We can overcome almost any problem with God's help and a little imagination. You may not sense God's strength, grace, and guidance right now. But He is never late. He'll be there just in time.

With a God who knows the way through and asks of us only that we follow, there isn't much room for bewilderment or defeat.

Things You Wouldn't Take a Million Dollars For

1. Life itself
2. Your eyesight
3. Good health
4. Family and Friends
5. Your hearing
6. Your freedom
7. Salvation and a clear conscience
8. A purpose and goal of achievement
9. A heavenly home to come
10. Memories of good things

Thank God, you're a multimillionaire.

Dr. Mendell Taylor

Sure Things

I. The testimony of the Lord is sure (Psa.19:7).
II. The punishment of the wicked is sure (Psa.9:17).
III. The punishment of the believer who falls into sin is sure.
IV. The future blessedness of all believers in Christ is sure (Ezek. 18:20).

V. The coming again of Jesus Christ for His church is absolutely sure.
VI. The return of the Lord with His church to reign upon earth is sure.

What Paul Found in Christ

I. He discovered a new God. He found a God of grace as well as a God of law.
II. He discovered a new Savior.
III. He experienced a new birth.
IV. He received a new heart and became a new creature.
V. He was a new man with a new sense of mastery.
VI. He received a new concern and a new motivation.
VII. He had a new relationship to everyone.
VIII. He had a new hope.

What Difference Does It Make?

1. It makes all the difference in the world whether man is immortal or not.
2. It makes all the difference whether there is a supreme God of infinite power, wisdom, and holiness.
3. It makes all the difference whether sin is truly repulsive and defiling.
4. It makes all the difference whether Jesus Christ is truly God our Savior and Redeemer.
5. It makes all the difference whether we have a hope of another life to come with its rewards for faithfulness.

St. Paul's Conversion
Acts 9

1. It was unexpected.
2. It occurred far away from his former labors.
3. It was sudden.
4. It was accompanied by new light.

5. It was preceded by conviction.
6. It brought him into submission to Christ.
7. It was not understood by those traveling with him.
8. It led to deep humiliation—even fasting.
9. It changed his whole life.
10. It enabled God to use him greatly to win others to Christ.

A Decade after Paul's Conversion

1. His short stay in Damascus
2. His three years in Arabia
3. His return to Damascus
4. His return to Jerusalem
5. His return to Tarsus—after about 6 years

Future Events

1. The Rapture
2. Revelation of the Antichrist
3. The Great Tribulation
4. Battle of Armageddon
5. The return of Christ (Rev.19:11)
6. Binding of Satan (Rev.20:1)
7. Millennial Reign (Zech.14)
8. Satan's Final Rebellion
9. The Last Judgment
10. The New Heaven and New Earth

The Early Church
Acts 2:42-47

1. It was a learning church.
2. It was a church of fellowship.
3. It was a praying church.
4. It was a sharing church.
5. It was a worshipping church.

6. It was a happy church.
7. It was a reverent church.
8. It was a church where things happened.
9. It was a church made up of people whom others could not help liking.

How We Know the Bible Is the Word of God

I. Fulfilled Prophecy

    A. The Birth of Christ
    B. Heir to the throne of David
    C. Soviet expansionism

II. The Unity of the Book (II Tim.3:16)

    A book on science ten years old is out of date.
    The Bible has no contradictions.

III. The Power of the Book—its influence
IV. The endurance of the Book—forever

Complaints against Jesus

I. Jesus went to eat with tax collectors, Matthew and Zachaeus.

    A. These men were outcasts who had to find friends wherever they could.
    B. There was no fellowship with tax collectors.

        1. Couldn't talk to them
        2. Couldn't go on a journey with them
        3, Couldn't even do business with them

    C. They were barred from the worship of the synagogue; they couldn't be a witness in court.

    D. To have a daughter marry one was like turning her over to a wild beast.
    E. They did not accept, or offer hospitality.
        By going to their homes to eat and sharing company with their friends, Jesus was defying the conventions of the day.
        The Scribes and Pharisees despised the common man; Jesus loved him.
II. Jesus and His disciples didn't observe the rules of fasting.
III. Jesus healed people on the Sabbath Day.
IV. Jesus allowed a leper to approach Him; He even touched a leper.
V.   Jesus claimed to be the Son of God.

The One-Talent Man
Matt. 25:13-30

The parable of the talents is given to enforce the exhortation: "Watch therefore."

Two of those receiving talents made a 100% gain. They received the same praise. The third man received condemnation.

1. He accepted his responsibility for the one talent.
2. He had all he was able to handle.
3. He did not use what he had.
4. He hid his talent.
5. He blamed someone else for his failure
6. He lost the one talent he had.
7. He lost his soul.

Preparation for the End

We ought to be

1. Industrious (Diligent)

2. Tied very loosely to temporal things
3. Living with eternity in view—not conformed to this world
4. Serving as good examples to neighbors and associates
5. Expecting the return of Christ

We ought to

1. Love one another
2. Serve one another
3. Encourage one another
4. Be courteous to one another
5. Set an example to one another
6. Forgive one another
7. Not to judge one another
8. Be subject to one another
9. Edify one another
10. Pray for one another

The Nature of God

I. God is a Spirit.
II. He is Eternal—without beginning or end.
III. He is an intelligent Being. Nothing is hidden from Him.

   A. He knows all things past, present, and future.
   B. He knows the hearts of men.
   C. His knowledge is infallible.
   D. His knowledge is not obtained through the medium of His creatures.

The Power of God

I. Introduction

   A. God cannot work contradictions.
   B. God cannot feel pain or be weary or die.

    C. God cannot deny Himself. He is faithful in His promises.

II. The power of God was displayed in the creation of all things.
III. His power is constantly displayed in the preservation of all things.
IV. The power of God is displayed in the work of redemption.
V. The power of God is displayed in the conversion of sinners.
VI. His power is displayed in the lives of His children.

To Live Is Christ

"For to me to live is Christ, and to die is gain"
Phil. 1:21

Since Paul was in prison awaiting trail, he had to face the fact that it was very uncertain whether he would live or die. To him it made no difference.

1. For Paul, Christ had been the *beginning of life*. On the Damascus Road it was as if he had begun life all over.
2. Christ had been the *continuing of life*.
3. Christ was the *end of life*, because, for Paul, it was towards His eternal presence that his life always led.
4. Christ was for him the *inspiration of life*.
5. Christ had given the *strength of life* to Paul. It was His grace that was made perfect in Paul's weakness.
6. For Paul, Christ was the *reward of life*; the only worthwhile reward was closer fellowship with Jesus.

Paul said that if Christ were taken out of life there would be nothing left.

Paul's desire to live is not for his own sake, but for the sake of those to whom he continued to minister.

It is not Paul's aim to know about Christ, but *to know Him* personally.

The Holy Spirit in the Book of Joel
Joel 2:28

Joel was the oldest of the prophets whose writings have come down to us.

Just as God gave to Habakkuk in one little verse the text of the whole gospel of salvation, so He gave Joel the text of the whole doctrine of the spirit.

Like a rainbow upon the storm cloud, like a gleam of sunshine out of a dark sky, like a blossom amid regions of eternal snow, so Joel's beautiful vision comes out of a great national catastrophe.

I. The personal coming of the Spirit is evident.

II. The abundance of the outpouring is very strongly expressed. The Hebrew word *pour* means a large effusion. God does not give some of the Spirit. He gives the Spirit in His infinite fullness.

III. The universal extent of the outpouring, "upon all flesh," is different. Prior to this the Spirit's manifestations had been confined to certain individuals and to a single nation.

IV. There was to be no distinction of age nor sex. He said, "young men" and "old men;" "sons and daughters."

V. All social classes and conditions were included: "Servants and handmaidens." There was no class in the Old Testament, but in the New Testament there was. For example, Onesimus and Philemon.

VI. Special gifts and manifestations accompany the Spirit's coming— prophesy, dreams and visions, special illumination.

VII. The coming of the Holy Ghost will bring salvation to all who are willing to receive Him.

Jesus Was Put to Death

1. Because He identified Himself with prophecy,
2. Because He forgave sins (Matt.9:28),
3. Because He set the needs of men above traditions of the Sabbath (John 5),
4. Because He offered Himself as the Bread of Life (John 6:22),
5. Because of His attitude toward a fallen woman,
6. Because of the violence with which He drove the moneychangers out of the Temple,
7. Because He visited with Zachaeus (Luke 19),
8. Because He thought more of the sanctity of life than the outward cleansing of hands,
9. Because He had wisdom beyond His schooling,
10. Because He raised Lazarus from death,
11. Because He received little children and blessed them.
12. Because He said that He was the Son of God.

Ultimately, of course, He was put to death to atone for our sins.

It might seem strange that God, watching the tragedy on Golgotha, should have done nothing. But He did do something! Remember the darkness? The earthquake? Dead ones coming forth from the grave? The veil torn in two?

In the book *Precious Bane*, Mary Webb tells of a poor woman with a great heart of love. She said, "It always seemed a strange thing to me that the mother of Jesus could keep her hands off the centurion in charge of the crucifixion—beating and scratching him; and it could only have been because her Son had given her orders some time before. But if it had been me," she said, "I think I'd have forgotten the orders!"

Someone once read the story of the death of Jesus to King Clovis, a barbarian. As the story went on, the king's hand reached for his sword. He said, "Oh, if only I had been there with my

Franks! We'd have charged the slopes of Calvary and smashed those Romans and saved Him!"

But we must remember that he could have saved Himself as the two thieves asked Him to do. Had He saved Himself, however, He could not have saved others. He died of His own volition to save the world.

The Importance of Jesus' Prayer
John 17:17

"Sanctify them through thy truth:
thy word is truth."

I. His last great high-priestly prayer before going to the cross

If the disciples could not be sanctified, Jesus preached something they could not live and prayed for something they could never have.

II. For whom was Jesus Praying?

   A. For Himself
   B. For His believing disciples
      There is abundant proof that these men were really saved or converted.
   C. For those that would believe through their works

III. Why did these disciples need to be sanctified?

   A. There was the fear of man when all forsook Jesus and fled.
   B. There was Thomas with his doubts.
   C. There was a lack of unity. Carnality is at the root of all church trouble.
   D. There was a "big I" and "little you" spirit among the group.
   E. There was a spirit of self-seeking.

IV. How and when did the disciples receive the experience Jesus prayed for them to have?

In Acts 2 we have the answer. After a period of waiting, praying, and soul-searching, they were in one accord in one place.

There was the Spirit that fills, the bond of love that unites, the wind that shakes, and the fire that purges.

What is Sanctification?

Sanctification is an act of God's grace by which inbred sin is removed and the heart made holy.

I. Inbred sin or inherited depravity is the inward cause of which our outward sins are the effects.
II. It is the bitter root of which actual sins are the bitter fruits.
III. It is the natural evil tendency of the human heart in our fallen condition.
IV. It is the being of sin which lies back of the doing of sin.
V. It is called in the New Testament

A. The flesh,
B. The body of sin,
C. The old man,
D. The sin that dwelleth in me,
E. Sin.

VI. In the Old Testament it is called "sin" and "iniquity" (Psa.51; Isa.6)
VII. Inbred sin goes back to the fall of man in the Garden of Eden.

But God has required His children to be holy in every age and dispensation. This means the destruction or removal of inbred sin.

What Is Sin?

Sin has baffled the skill of the ages. Human remedies without number have been tried. But when sin in one form has been checked, it has broken out in another form in a new, or perhaps in the same, place.

Sin is so subtle that it gets by the most vigilant detective; so deep-seated that the surgeon's knife cannot remove it; and so deadly that the strongest cannot survive it. It conquered Samson, the strong, and Absalom, the fair, and Solomon, the wise.

I. Wrong Concepts of Sin

    A. Modern psychology gives us no place for sin. The notable psychiatrist, Dr. Karl Menninger wrote *What Ever Happened to Sin?* According to modern psychology we should follow our instincts and desires because any thwarted instinct cramps and limits our personality.

        But the laws of every land restrain and restrict men from following their instincts, for in many cases these instincts are destructive.

    B. Christian Science defines sin as error. It practically denies sin's existence.

    C. Many try to minimize sin. They think it is not really so bad after all. They claim that we can never be made free from it.

    D. Some would glorify sin.

    E. The only right attitude is to fear and forsake sin.

II. The True Definition of Sin

    A. Sin is the transgression of the law (I John 3:4). Dr. Ponder Gilliland defines sin as "the voluntary violation of a known law of God by a morally responsible person."

B. "To him that knoweth to do good and doeth it not, to him it is sin" (James 4:17). In other words, sin is failing to do my known duty, either to God, to myself, or to my fellowman.

   A negative religion is not enough. It is no self-evident fact that you will to go heaven simply because you never killed anybody or did anything you thought worldly or sinful.

C. "Whatsoever is not of faith is sin" (Rom. 14:22-23).

   In everyday language this means that whatever I cannot do with a clear conscience is sin to me. Under these circumstances what is sin to one person may not be sin to another.

D. "All unrighteousness is sin" (I John 5:17).

   Everything unholy. Not only is it wrong to do the things that are sinful, but the purposes, motives, inner thoughts of the heart may be sinful as well.

Holiness as a Second Work of Grace
I Peter 3:15

I. All churches, as far as I know, have sanctification in their doctrine. We differ in the way and time it is received or obtained.

   A. At the time of conversion—all-at-once theory
   B. By growing into the experience—the growth theory
   C. At death—dying grace theory
   D. In purgatory or by sacraments
   E. As a second work of grace

II. Different terms are used in Scripture to describe this experience.

   A. Perfect love
   B. Baptism with the Holy Spirit

    C. Abundant life
    D. Christian perfection
    E. Holiness
    F. Crucified life
    G. Sanctification

        1. To consecrate
        2. To make holy

III. What sanctification is not

    A. Absolute
    B. Angelic
    C. Abnormal
    D. Physical
    E. Mental
    F. Ethical

IV. What sanctification is
    It is a perfection of

    A. Love
    B. Heart
    C. Nature
    D. Affection

Why I Believe in Sanctification

I. It is an experience for this life. Luke 1:74-75 says, " . . . that we being delivered out of the hands of our enemies might serve him without fear, in holiness and righteousness, before him, all the days of our life."

II. It is not a new thing. "According as he hath chosen us in him before the foundation of the world, that we should be holy and without blame before him in love" (Eph. 1:4).

III. It is nothing to be ashamed of. "For both he that

sanctifieth, and they who are sanctified, are all of one, for which cause he is not ashamed to call them brethren" (Heb. 2:11).

IV. It is God's will for us.

    A. "For this is the will of God, even your sanctification . . ." (I Thes.4:3).
    B. "By the which will we are sanctified through the offering of the body of Jesus Christ once for all" (Heb.10:10).

V. It is His promise. "And, behold, I send the promise of my Father upon you: but tarry ye in Jerusalem until ye be endued with power from on high" (Luke 24:49).

VI. It is His command. "Because it is written; be ye holy for I am holy" (I Peter 1:16).

VII. It cleanses from all sin. "And put no difference between us and them, purifying their hearts by faith" (Acts 15:9).

VIII. It is the burden of the prayer of Jesus in John 17:17, 20. "Sanctify them" and "all that shall believe on me through their word."

IX. It prepares us for heaven and the second coming.

    A. "Blessed are the pure in heart: for they shall see God" (Matt.5:8).
    B. "Follow peace with all men, and holiness, without which no man shall see the Lord." (Heb.12:14).
    C. "And the very God of peace sanctify you wholly; and I pray God your whole spirit and soul and body be preserved blameless unto the coming of our Lord Jesus Christ" (I Thes. 5:23).

X. It was the purpose of His death.

    A. "Wherefore Jesus also that he might sanctify the people with his own blood suffered without the gate" (Heb.13:12).

B. "Husbands, love your wives as Christ also loved the church and gave himself for it; that he might sanctify and cleanse it, with the washing of water by the word" (Eph. 5:26-27).

When the Music Starts
Dan. 3

Three young men in Babylon refused to conform.

1. There is always peer pressure to go along, to bow down too when everybody's doing it.
2. There must come a time when we make up our minds as to what God we will serve, or bow down to. If everybody's doing it, why should I be an odd ball? If people we look up to think it's all right, then it must be all right—or is it?
3. These three young men—Shadrach, Meshach, and Abednego—had settled it ahead of time that they would be true to God.
4. We are always in danger of being forced into the mold of the age.
5. We must decide what is important enough to stake our all on. What kind of God for me? What kind of lifestyle for me?
6. The idol was impressive and the consequences for not worshipping it were deadly. But the three Hebrew children refused to bow down. And the God that they served refused to let them down.

Eternity—Where Will You Spend It?
Eccl.12:5

The word "eternity" is found only once in the Bible. Yet it is the most important of all considerations. More people think about this subject than we realize. The headline "Student Ends

Life to Find What Is beyond Death" could no doubt be repeated again and again. Of course, we would all like to know more about the hereafter. But all we know for sure is what the Bible tells us. That should be enough to persuade us to prepare for it.

I. There is an Eternity. It is the mark of a very shallow person to be thoughtless about it.
II. We must spend that Eternity somewhere. We may try to close our eyes to this fact, but it still stands. Ten thousand years from now we will be in a conscious existence somewhere.
III. The question where I spend Eternity is much more important than how I spend the present. Suppose I live in a shack, suffer hunger, and wear rags in this life. Suppose I live in a mansion, fare sumptuously, and drive a Rolls Royce. Either condition is temporary. What really matters is where I go when I die. That choice is up to me.
IV. It is possible for us to know where we will spend Eternity.
   Some think it's all a guess. But the Bible clearly teaches that there is a heaven prepared for those who accept Christ and a hell for those who reject Him.
V. We will spend Eternity in one of two places.
   The location of these places is not important. The character is.
   Heaven means holiness, happiness, love, joy, freedom from trouble or pain, the presence of departed loved ones who died in the faith, everything the heart yearns for, and best of all, the presence of the Lord we've loved and served across the years.
   Hell means eternal damnation, violence, torture, hate, despair, separation from God.
VI. Where you will spend Eternity will be settled in this life.
   Our Eternal destiny is settled in this life by our own deliberate choices. We get no second chance.
   "Preacher," someone asked, "Where is hell?"

The answer? "At the end of a sinful life."
VII. Where you spend Eternity will be determined by what you do with Jesus now.

No one needs to be lost for all Eternity because Jesus will save "whosoever will" follow Him (Rev. 22: 17).

The Purposes of Calvary

"And I, if I be lifted up from the earth, will
draw all men unto me (John 12:32).

I. Christ died that we might have a Divine Demonstration.

   A. "But God commendeth his love toward us, in that, while we were yet sinners, Christ died for us. Much more then, being now justified by his blood, we shall be saved from wrath through him" (Rom. 5: 8-9).
   B. "But ye are a chosen generation, a royal priesthood, an holy nation, a peculiar people; that ye should shew forth the praises of him who hath called you out of darkness into his marvelous light" (I Peter 2:9).

   If the attitude of an individual toward Calvary is wrong, it is impossible for him to think straight about other things. Heaven or hell results from an attitude. A wrong attitude is a rejection of God's overtures, God's method, and God's love.

II. Christ died that we might have a New Destiny (I Peter 3:18).

   A. It was necessary that we be brought to God.
   B. All men are not sons of God.
   C. By His death we can be transformed from the sons of the devil to the sons of God. Thus we can choose heaven and escape hell.

III. Christ died that we might have a New Deliverance.

   A. The greatest need of a sin-cursed humanity can be expressed in one word "deliverance."
   B. The power of sin makes deliverance impossible in our human efforts.
   C. Calvary alone provides the aid from God that deliverance requires.

IV. Christ died that we might have a New Desire (II Cor.5:15).

   A. The vast majority of human impulses are selfish. We need an incentive to turn from sin.
   B. Christ died that the whole motive of our lives might be changed.
   C. Christ's death gives us the privilege of investing our lives in His kingdom.

V. Christ died to give us a New Dynamic. "But ye shall receive power, after that the Holy Ghost is come upon you: and ye shall be witnesses unto me both in Jerusalem, and in all Judaea, and in Samaria, and unto the uttermost part of the earth" (Acts 1:8).

   A. He gives us a power geared to a purpose.
   B. The purpose is to raise men above the level of sin and to empower us to live for Christ.

VI. Christ died that we might have a New Dominion. "For none of us liveth to himself, and no man dieth to himself. For whether we live, we live unto the Lord; and whether we die, we die unto the Lord: whether we live therefore, or die, we are the Lord's. For to this end Christ both died, and rose, and revived, that he might be Lord both of the dead and living" (Rom.14:7-9).

CHAPTER 4

Sermons

Unbelief

One obstacle stands in the way of the mighty works of Christ. That obstacle is unbelief.

He could turn water into wine. He could command the storm-swept sea into perfect calm. He could multiply a boy's meager lunch into an abundant feast for thousands of hungry people. He could make crippled people leap for joy. He could make sick ones rise up from their bed of suffering. He could make the deaf to hear, the blind to see, and even the dead to live again. But He could not do many such works when the atmosphere about Him was charged with stubborn unbelief.

Go back in your imagination to a scene outside the village church in Nazareth. A young Man has come home and preached. Because He was wise without being learned, because He was spiritually powerful, and because He was nobody but one of themselves, they were ready to show their doubts about Him. "And He marveled because of their unbelief" (Mark 6:6).

Their unbelief was the rejection of spiritual power in the plain face of that power. It was the refusal to recognize and to accept a spiritual power whose force was visible to them where they could all see it. They were not asked to accept something they could not see.

Unbelief is very popular today. Probably no other generation has paid such a high honor to unbelief as has ours. Today we think unbelief means intellectual unwillingness to accept—or swallow—ancient doctrines. But there is no doctrine here.

What is unbelief?

1. It is the spirit of "It can't be done." Treating any situation as though it could never be remedied questions God's ability to remedy a hopeless situation or solve an impossible problem.
2. It is unbelief when you are called upon to assume a responsibility and you say, "No, I'm not capable of doing that; I know I'd fail." We use only 15% of our capabilities.
3. It is unbelief when we are called to go through something and we waver and fear. We can believe in miracles in the New Testament and in the Old, but not in our own lives.
4. It is unbelief to be satisfied with second best when we can aim at first. We stop short or give up too soon.
5. It is unbelief when we see the power of God come wonderfully down into the life of another, and we say, "But that could never happen to me!" How do you know it couldn't?

Lift up your eyes to Christ and lay hold of every meaning you can find in Him. Bring to Him, not only yourself, but your problems; not only your faith, but your unbelief as well, praying with the centurion of old, "Lord, I believe, help thou my unbelief."

When Jesus appeared to the eleven after His resurrection, He upbraided them for their unbelief and hardness of heart. But He would not rebuke an honest intellectual dissent.

Unbelief is the negative atmosphere, the unexpectant, hopeless attitude. It causes us to think people—especially those we know best, whose lives seem to be so set—can never be altered.

Unbelief is acting and feeling as though there were no God in the daily conduct of our lives.

When a spiritual leader dreams great dreams for his group

and sees in them a great spiritual center, where men and women may see the living Christ held up and feel the Spirit among them, where people are finding Christ and being forever truly changed, going out to be a blessing, someone says, "Don't expect too much; that's a daydream you have. These people will not really get what you mean. They will be just like every other crowd of church people—no friendlier, no deeper, no better. Don't expect too much!" That is unbelief.

Discovering What Religion Is All About

" . . . and what doth the Lord require of thee,
but to do justly, and to love mercy, and to walk
humbly with thy God?" (Micah 6:8)

Every one of us has a religion we live by whether we realize it or not.

When pressed for a definition of religion, however, some have trouble putting it into words; others could do it immediately.

Religion is that which gives unity and direction and power to our lives. It is that about which we get excited and from which we derive the greatest strength for living; something we struggle for, and, if need be, die for.

There are only two great realities in the universe, the fact of God and the heart of man. Each is constantly seeking the other. The religious history of mankind is the story of this two-way seeking and of the ways that men have used in times past, and use today, to bring about a meeting of the two.

Basically, religion has to do with a joining together of God and man. The word *religion* is derived from a Latin term which means "to bind." So religion could be thought of as that which binds God and man. It binds us to God, to our fellow man in a fellowship of things immortal, and to ourselves into a unified, integrated personality.

When we reduce life to its bare essentials, we find there is only one thing really needful—to know God and to possess Him.

There are three approaches to spiritual reality: belief, worship, and behavior.

William Law defines religion as a triad of authority, reason, and experience forming a "Three-fold cord that cannot be easily broken."

In the book of Micah we find the best and most concise description of religion. ". . . what doth the Lord require of thee, but to do justly, and to love mercy, and to walk humbly with thy God" (Micah 6:8). These words are carved on the entrance of one of the greatest and oldest institutions in our eastern United States. They remind us that religion, in its basic form, is not a system, nor a creed, nor a ritual; it is a quiet, honest way of living before God and man a life of righteousness, of justice, mercy, and love.

1. Christianity is primarily a message from God and about God.

   God, out of His mercy, and on His own initiative, has acted for man's deliverance from the tyranny of sin and death.

   Man, by searching and seeking, could not otherwise get to God.

   God has not left us alone. He cares for us with a love passing human understanding.

   Jesus never used the word *religion*. The word He used instead was *life*. If men accept God's gift to them in Christ, then the religion of Christ becomes eternal life in the midst of time, by the strength and under the eyes of God.

   We could go on to a study of the gospel accounts and come up with this: We want to follow in Jesus' steps, trust in God, obey His will, and rest in the Lord. This is the heart of Christianity. This is what it's all about. To these words I should add gratitude to God for His being Who He is and doing what He has done and is doing to bring about our salvation.

2. This great salvation is a constant exchange of material we cannot keep for riches we cannot lose.
3. What is religion all about?

There is Jesus' definition—Life. Brother Lawrence's definition is "living continually in the presence of God." Albert Schweitzer's definition is "reverence for life, all life." Dr. James B. Chapman defined it as "a creed to be believed, a life to be lived, and an experience to be enjoyed." These are only a few of the many interpretations that wise and holy men have come to accept through the years.

Suppose we say that religion is a matter of vertical and horizontal, with its center in one's self. It must have an upward thrust, linking us with the timeless, eternal life of God. It must be an outward movement, serving our fellow men in their needs as we see those needs.

There must be, at the heart, real integrity and purity in our lives. There must be reverence and adoration, sympathy and service, personal holiness and soul purity. Beyond these, we cannot go, and short of them, we dare not stop.

To try to make our Christian faith a comforting cult is a sure sign of a sick generation. To have Christ is the mystery of a power, a personality, and a presence.

Christianity and Your Life
Matt. 21:33-41

The dramatic and vivid parable we read here is the story of a highly favored nation that failed to realize God's purpose.

Writers have commented on the drastic and impossible conduct of those husbandmen. But it is not safe to argue from conditions such as we know in modern America.

In Palestine, especially in Galilee, at the time of Christ, there was considerable unrest, and it is not unthinkable that the refusal to pay rent might be the thing that would trigger a murder and the forcible seizure of land by the peasantry. Various writers tell us that this kind of thing often happened in Galilee during the half-century preceding the general revolt of A.D.66.

The Vineyard is the prophetic symbol for the Jewish nation. As Jesus painted this word picture, He had in mind the Jews who were listening to Him. It is recorded that "he spake of them" (v.45). But since a nation is made of individuals, the story is essentially one of human life.

The more we read this parable, the more evident it becomes that this represents the story of your life and mine.

Let's follow it verse by verse and mark, learn, and inwardly digest the many serious lessons that are found here.

I. The Privileges of Your Life
   A. God likens your life to a vineyard to which He has given much thought and care. As the Divine Householder, he has planted the vineyard.

   Have you ever paused to consider the story of your coming into the world? But for God's forethought and care, you would never have been planted—or born. You owe your very existence to Him. Behind your parents and secondary causes, there is the hand of your Creator. Medical science today acknowledges that physical birth is still the greatest miracle of human life. Without God's forethought and care, it could never happen.
   B. As we follow the story we learn further that the vineyard was "hedged about." Perhaps you have never realized that but for the fact of God's protecting care you wouldn't be alive. From the cradle to the grave, life is one long battle against disease, decay, sin, and unseen forces of evil. Looking back upon my life, I have to thank God again and again for His protecting care.
   C. Then the Divine Householder "digged a wine-vat." God's goodness is such that He has provided you with the capacity to receive and reciprocate—as far

as it is humanly possible—all His good gifts. And so the Apostle Paul reminds us that "God giveth us richly all things to enjoy." The "all things" include the temporal mercies and spiritual blessings that God showers upon us day by day for our personal enjoyment.

D. Finally, we notice His preserving care: He "built a tower. The tower was the look-out from which enemies within the vineyard could be detected.

Here is another way God has expressed His loving care for us. We have the inner tower of Conscience, so we can discern between good and evil. "This is the true light that lighteth every man that cometh into the world" (John 1:9). The fact that you have not heeded the warnings of Conscience is no reflection on God's care.

II. The Purpose of Your Life

The purpose of your life is set forth in these words: "He let the vineyard out to husbandmen . . . that he might receive the fruits of it." When one comes to the age of responsibility, God lets out the life for the cultivation of fruit. The fruit He expects is righteousness. This is clear from reading Isaiah 5, from which our Lord quoted this parable.

Jesus sums up the message in Mark 12:30-31: "And thou shalt love the Lord thy God with all thy heart, and with all thy soul, and with all thy mind, and with all thy strength: this is the first commandment. Thou shalt love thy neighbor as thyself."

A. The purpose of your life is to yield to Him the fruit of unconditional love. To love God with all your heart means more than mere lip service or nominal living. This means loving God with a heart that has been transformed, regenerated, and indwelt by the

Holy Spirit, for "the fruit of the Spirit is love . . ." (Gal. 5:22).

1. That purpose includes giving to God the fruit of your emotional love. "Thou shalt love the Lord thy God with all thy soul." This involves loving God in such a way that everybody will know it; all can see it, feel it, and hear it.
2. God expects the fruit of your enlightened love. "Thou shalt love the Lord thy God . . . with all thy mind."
   This presupposes time spent in getting to know God

   a. By studying His Word,
   b. By engaging in prayer,
   c. By developing a regular church life,
   d. By Christian devotion.

3. God expects the fruit of your energetic love. "Thou shalt love the Lord thy God . . . with all thy strength."
   Having rendered to God His due, you are ready to fulfill the second great purpose of your life.

B. The second purpose of your life is to yield social judgment and righteousness. The extension of the first commandment socially affects our fellow men for good.

C. The further purpose for your life is to yield self judgment and righteousness—Jesus says, "Love thy neighbor as thyself." He doesn't say, "better than thyself."

We are to love God and man so that the effect of such loving destroys selfishness, while it develops selflessness in us.

What a high and holy purpose God has designed for your life! He has planted you as a vineyard with this thought in mind. You belong to God. He has a right to expect something of you.

III. The Prerogative of Your Life

The most amazing thing about your life is that, even though God has blessed you with privilege and purpose, you have the prerogative to ignore Him or to acknowledge Him. God gives you the opportunity to exercise your moral power of choice.

A. You can ignore God by misusing His sovereignty. You owe all to God, but you may not acknowledge His claims on your life.
B. You can further ignore God by abusing His servants.

We read that "the husbandmen took the servants, and beat one, killed another, and stoned another." This abusing of God's servants is always characteristic of those who will not acknowledge the claims of God upon their lives.

Analyze the feelings that rise up within you when God's servants challenge your life. If there are emotions of enmity and hostility, you should realize that you are virtually beating, stoning, and killing God's servants.

And what should I say about the times when they and their sermons are criticized before the children?

C. More than all else, you can ignore God by refusing His Son.

The parable reminds us that the husbandmen "took him, and killed him and cast him out of the vineyard." This is the greatest sin anyone can commit. In a very real way it means "crucifying the Son of God afresh, and putting him to an open shame" (Heb. 6:6). Is it any wonder that the story closes with the destruction of those who did such a crime as to murder the Owner's Son?

Jesus was giving His autobiography. Six days later it happened as He said it would.

Think again of the privileges of your life and of the high purposes of your life. Surely such considerations demand the right use of your prerogative of choice.

Recognize God's sovereignty by yielding to Him the fruit of your life. Most of all, receive God's Son by inviting Him into the vineyard of your life. Then the privileges of your life will be justified, the purpose of your life will be ratified, and the prerogative of your life will be satisfied.

The Five Foolish Virgins
(Matt.25:1-13)

"Five were foolish." What a striking and shocking statement! If Jesus had told of five old men who had long since sown to the wind and were reaping the whirlwind, it would sound much more logical. But five foolish virgins?

They thought they were prepared. They had lamps just like the wise virgins. Had everything gone as they expected, they would have been prepared. But does anything ever go according to expectations?

How strikingly the two groups resemble in every way, yet how far apart Jesus puts them!

Jesus did not tell what excuses may have been in the minds or on the lips of the five foolish virgins. But that is one good feature about a parable. We can fill in our own picture from imagination and experience.

I. Possibly one of the foolish virgins had the idea that her lamp was a symbol of welcome. She was trusting in her lamp.

  A. A lamp is a lamp whether it's lighted or not.
  B. All one needs is good intentions.

II. The second was willing to carry a lamp because a lamp was beautiful and she might need it. But carrying a jug of oil might spoil her garments and maybe cause a stench. She was concerned about her appearance.

III. The third bought only what oil she thought was necessary. She would not buy extra oil which might not be used. She was thrifty.
IV. The fourth was quite certain there would be no delay. With her small amount of oil, her lamp would be lighted and she could go into the wedding feast. She would be on time. She would have enough oil in her lamp if the wedding party moved according to schedule. Her attitude was one of presumption.
   Trouble might come to other people, but not to her.
V. Perhaps the fifth maiden entertained the thought that her lamp might possibly go out since she wasn't carrying an extra vessel of oil. But, if it did, she would creep up close to the others and manage to get in. If her oil burned out, there would be other lamps burning to cover her fault. One unlighted lamp wouldn't be noticed. Even if it was, the good man of the house would be considerate. He would say, "O well, let her in."

Oil was the one necessity that night. It was not lamps, however beautiful or symbolic.

If any one of these young women had suspected that she would find herself unprepared for such an emergency, she would doubtless have checked her oil before she left home.

The Foolishness of Preaching
(I Cor.1:21)

The foolishness of preaching was to those of Paul's day the preaching of foolishness.

Rome knew too much about world conquering to think that such a thing could be done by a king who was already dead and had not left even a sword in the hands of His followers.

To the Greek, who sought after culture, it seemed the height of folly to point them away from Plato's ideals of the good and the beautiful and to bid them look for God in a man who was born in a stable, nailed to a tree, and died the accursed death of a Hebrew criminal.

But what the wisdom of the world failed to do down through the ages the foolishness of preaching has been accomplishing because it has been the power of God unto salvation to all that believe.

Men began to see that the cross was the way to God. Even Julian, the Apostate, who spent his whole lifetime in a vain attempt to crush it, was forced to cry in his dying hour, "Galilean, Thou hast conquered!"

In the best that the world's wisdom can do, you will search in vain for the teaching that man's sin has alienated him from God, for any such thing as atonement, free forgiveness, or regenerating grace.

Philosophy might, and did, point men to God as an intellectual concept. But, to a God of salvation—for the knowledge of Whom the world was dying—the world with all its boasted science and philosophy could not point the way, for "The world by wisdom knew not God," we're told.

We're not surprised, therefore, to find that the old civilization with its philosophy and its customs bore its ripest fruit in a sea of corruption and a cesspool of licentiousness and iniquity.

Marriage was a farce, virtue a mockery, chastity on sale, and purity a thing unknown.

Men and women were set on fire of hell and the wisdom of this world was as powerless as a child trying to stem the Niagara dam with toothpicks or corn cobs.

This was the awful condition of life when Jesus came into the world and the Cross of Christ dawned like the morning star over this great sea of darkness. It was into this putrid mass of moral decay that Christianity was to pour its purifying current of the knowledge of the One who alone was able to redeem it.

And across the centuries this mighty gulf stream of salvation has poured through the waste lands of this sin-cursed world to a perishing humanity without God and without hope.

The world has been longing for a knowledge of God like this—a religion whose central idea was love and which centered about the life of One who so loved that He gave His life a ransom for men, a religion that offered an escape from the evils of the day by a power mightier than their own, a remedy for the sins that held them captive.

The Gospel of Christ through the centuries has done that very thing. Christ is marching on!

How utterly futile to attempt to hold back the life-giving tides of a religion like this! You might as well sit on the shore of the mighty ocean, like old King Canute, and bid the tide stay back, or command the sun not to shine.

What Julian the Apostate said, many others have had to say, "O, Galilean, Thou hast conquered." The whole world will have to say that when the knowledge of the Lord fills the earth as the waters cover the sea and every tongue shall confess that Christ is Lord to the glory of God.

The news media implies that Christianity has failed because it has not prevented crime, terror, and wars. But suppose most of these nations have been engaged during the past generation or two in trying to destroy and obliterate Christianity. Suppose the news media, the theater, and the government have often been in a conspiracy to dethrone Christ and extinguish the fires of spirituality.

Suppose the evils of which we complain are the direct result of crowding out of our daily public and private lives the principles of Christian conduct. Oh, we're quick to recognize God and pray to Him in time of trouble. In case of disaster we take it for granted that every victim went straight to heaven regardless of the way he/she had lived.

If you become seriously ill after disobeying the doctor's orders, will you blame the physician? Yet many people have rejected the Great Physician and scorned His remedies, and now they blame Him because He has not kept them from trouble.

Christianity has not failed mankind; rather men have failed Christ. The final judgment will reveal who is foolish.

A Fool's Five Mistakes
Luke 12:16-21

"Thou fool!" Jesus frowns upon our using such language. But He used it on this occasion of a rich man who was evidently mentally sound. Why did Jesus call him a fool?

Not because he has been successful or because he is rich. Not because he accumulated his money dishonestly. Evidently he made his money legitimately by farming. Not because he was trying to save what he made. Nor does he want to waste it in loose living. What is wrong?

I. He left God out of his life. He probably wasn't an atheist, but he lived as if the fact of God were an absolute lie.

    A. He had no sense of Divine ownership.
    B. He had no sense of obligation.
    C. He confused possession and ownership.
    D. He had no sense of gratitude.

II. He left man out of his thinking. The only pronouns in his vocabulary are "I," "My," and "Mine."

III. He tried to feed his soul on things—"much goods." He undertook to treat his soul as he would treat his sheep and his goats. An immortal soul can never be fed corn or wheat or hay. It is satisfied only be eternal values.

IV. He thought that riches meant ease. "Take thine ease . . . Be merry," he says to his soul. Obviously all his riches had not satisfied his hungry soul in the past.

    Riches never satisfy. One-third of the parables of Jesus have to do with man and his possessions.

V. He thought he had a lease on life, " . . . many years," but he had a wrong conception of eternity.

    He was a fool for failing no make provision for eternity. Man says, "Many years." God says, "This night."

Spiritual Warfare

We are, whether we know it or not, fighting on three fronts: the world, the flesh, and the devil.

The history of the world is in reality an outward manifestation of the unseen warfare between God and Satan. The Bible gives us the record of this conflict in its past, present, and future.

In the beginning there was God alone, self-sufficient and perfect. God created the magnificence of heaven and populated the universe with great hosts of spirit beings we call angels.

Over them God set Lucifer, who acted as prime minister of the universe. He was God's prophet, speaking for God. As God's priest and representative, he ruled the universe for Him. He was full of wisdom and perfect in beauty.

And then, somehow Lucifer got the idea that he could run everything without God. [He still puts that idea into our heads]. He declared his independence, and a certain number of the angelic host broke away with him.

The scene of this rebellion was apparently planet Earth. If so, it explains why this tiny speck of dust amid all the heavenly galaxies is the stage for the drama of the ages.

In response to Satan's challenge, God sent judgment on the earth, and it became "without form, and void," and darkness covered the face of the deep.

It was as though God said, "Lucifer, you have become Satan"—or Adversary. "You claim that you can run the universe without Me. There is your earth, and it is all chaos now, so show your power by unscrambling it."

And God gave Satan thousands, perhaps millions, of years in which to restore the earth.

When Satan's inability had been completely exposed, God stepped in.

The power of His word accomplished what Satan could not do. The earth was refashioned, reformed, and remodeled. Then He created Adam and Eve.

When Satan saw man placed over the realm that had once

been his, he reasoned that if he could get man to disobey God, the Creator would have nothing to do with man.

Of course God knew the plans of Satan and had already prepared the pattern of salvation that would bring all mankind back to Himself and produce harmony once again.

God made the provision; man makes his decision.

A Soldier of Christ

"Thou therefore endure hardness as a good soldier of Jesus Christ."
II Tim. 2:3

I. Christian life is warfare. There never was such a war.

    A. Some wars have lasted thirty years; this one has been raging at least six centuries.
    B. Some wars involve several nations; this one has penetrated three or more worlds.
    C. The forces in earthly battles rarely exceed two or three million. In this war every angel and every human being participates.
    D. Most wars result in changes of government in cities and countries involved; this war results in salvation from damnation.

II. This war calls for volunteers. Christ issues a call for volunteers to enlist on His side. He never drafts anyone.

III. In this war there can be no substitute. In civil war men may pay another to go fight in their place. The substitute stands, marches, and sometimes dies in the battle.
In Christian warfare some look for substitutes.

    A. Some men make their wives their substitutes.
    B. Others use their preachers and priests.
    C. Some even use money.

But such efforts are in vain.

IV. In this war there can be no furlough. The U.S. army gives a leave of absence for sickness, important business matters, or a chance to relax and visit with loved ones. But in God's army the battle is always on. No one can be spared.

When a Christian worker takes a few weeks of rest from regular duties, he is not on furlough; he is still serving God.

The story is told of St. Francis and a young student. St. Francis suggested they walk through a city. When the student asked why, the old saint said, "To preach." But all they did was walk.

As they left, the student said, "You said we came to preach."

St. Francis said, "We did. We have been preaching all the time."

What about one who shirks his duty? He excuses himself from responsibility. He gives up church, prayer meeting, Sunday school, and family prayer. He is AWOL. Punishment is imminent.

V. In this war there can be no discharge. We enlist for a lifetime. Some of the fiercest battles may be fought in youth, but there will be some equally as trying in middle and old age.

We are vulnerable though we have won a thousand victories. To be faithful for fifty years and unfaithful the fifty-first year is to go down in defeat like a ship that, having sailed around the world and weathered scores of storms, strikes a rock and goes down in sight of home port.

VI. In this war we may expect hard times. It is neither a picnic nor a holiday. We will face persecutions, disappointments, misunderstandings, pain, self-denial, and loneliness.

VII. In this war we do not always know the plans of the Captain. "His ways are past finding out." But it is enough for us to obey. Since the Lord knows the way through the wilderness, all we have to do is to follow.
VIII. In this war our Captain is bound to win. This cannot be said of any other, but Christ has all power! Hell trembles before Him.

   Jesus is sure to win. Sinners apprehend it. Devils know it. The Bible teaches it. Christians feel it and rejoice in it.

The kingdoms of this world shall become the kingdoms of our Lord, and His Christ.

Amen and amen. Even so come, Lord Jesus!

The Weapons of Gideon
Judges 7:16-22

Gideon made the mistake of looking first at the enemy; next at himself; last at God.

The Lord gave him three signs to arouse in him the spirit of faith and fearlessness: (1) the wet fleece; (2) the dry fleece; (3) God's permission to go to the camp of the Midianites and hear what they were saying.

Gideon had only 30,000 men, yet God said that was too many. By various processes He sifted them down to only 300.

I. When victory came, men could see that it was not by human might, but by divine intervention.

   A. The only explanation was that God was with Gideon and his 300 men. He touched the things in their hands and transformed them into weapons of omnipotence.
   B. Of course it is God who wins the battle. But He relies on man to do his part.

II. Every man stood in his place.

   A. Here was a concert of action, and above all, individual faithfulness. This was not a disorganized mob.
   B. There is always a place of duty where God wants us to be.
   C. There was never a great work done for souls, but that a certain number of men stood in their places.

II. "They blew their trumpets."

   A. The effect was terrifying.
   B. This represents our testimony. In this case everyone blew his own horn, but God used their efforts

III. Gideon's band "broke their pitchers."

   A. This signifies that these bodies of ours must be given up and, if need be, sacrificed for the cause of truth and righteousness.
   B. There is such a thing as spending and being spent in the service of the Lord. The blood of the martyrs became the seed of the church. Their pitchers were broken.

IV. The men waved their lanterns.

   A. We too must let our lights shine.
   B. The lantern is to go with the trumpet. Our lives must follow up and confirm our testimony.

V. The men presented a united front. A trumpet, a broken pitcher, a waving lantern means individual faithfulness; ringing testimony; the body of sacrifice; and the life luminous with the truth and the indwelling spirit of God.

God doesn't always do things the way we would. He disregards the host for the few. But cooperating with God always brings victory.

Gideon gave God credit for the victory even before it was won, but he did not fold his hands and say it was already done.

Power to Become
John 1:12

Power to become! We do not always have to be what we are. God makes available to us the power to become. Most of us are interested in *doing* of course. But *being* comes first.

The good news is that those who believe in Christ and accept Him as Lord can receive power to become children of God in a personal and joyous relationship.

John Wesley spent many years as a very proper, very formal, and very unhappy religionist. He was a fellow of Oxford University and a clergyman in the Church of England. But in 1738, when he was thirty-five years old, something happened at Aldersgate. From that day forward things were different.

Later, he wrote, "I had the faith of a *servant* but not the faith of a *son*.

God wants us to be sons and daughters—His own dear children.

I. Christian faith is based on a gift, not on a deal.

   A. God gave His Son. Christ, the Son, gave Himself. The Apostle Paul, writing to the Romans, said "the gift of God is eternal life."
   B. Jesus said, "Fear not, little flock, for it is the Father's good pleasure to give you the kingdom." We are not able to think in terms of having things like kingdoms given to us.

II. Our Christian faith operates on *love* not *law*.

    A. Laws are necessary for people who have no better motive for behaving themselves. Merely obeying a bunch of rules isn't generally known as the most thrilling experience in life!
    B. Christian life is not a set of rules; it's a love affair! Some people see it as just a moral code. Of course, it's better to live by a moral code than nothing at all.

III. Christian faith results in freedom, not enslavement.

    A. There are strait-jacket religions in the world, but Christianity is not one of them. Religions such as those may keep you out of jail, but usually they won't put much joy in your heart.
    B. We have freedom in Christ because we belong to Him.
    C. If the Christian life begins when we accept Christ as Savior, it continues as we follow Him as Lord. If a person's religion doesn't make him a better person, he needs a better religion.
    D. We are not yet what we may become. God is working on us, trying to conform us to the image of His Son. If we are going to receive from God, we must be willing to accept what He has to give and to receive it on His terms, not ours.

As His child each of us is unique, original, and very special to God. He has the power and the will to give us victory if we trust and obey Him.

The Chronology of Creation Events

When God made this earth He established a place where a creature called man was going to be tested. Before man was created, however, God restored the earth from the chaotic condition caused by Satan's rebellion and brought forth life in the form of animals, fish, and fowl to inhabit the earth.

Some scholars believe that God created the world in six stages, six intervals separated by long periods of time. This is called the "age-day theory."

Another theory centers upon the concept that Genesis Chapters 1 and 2 describe an original and recent—in relationship to eternity—creation of the world.

I believe that Chapters 1 and 2 do not explain the original creation of Planet Earth and the universe, but assume their prior existence. If we take this view, these two chapters describe a *reconstruction* of the earth and its solar system and galaxies by God in six literal days.

Job 38:4-7 seems to indicate that God created this material universe before the angelic revolt and, of course, before the appearance of man. Job 38: 4 says, "Where were you when I laid the foundations of the earth?" Then he continues to speak of the great acts of creation.

In verse 7 Job continues, "When the morning stars sang together and the sons of God shouted for joy?" This statement undoubtedly refers to angels. It shows us that all the angelic beings were in harmony as they shouted for joy at this demonstration of God's great power.

Two important facts are brought out here:

1. The earth was created after the angels were and yet before the angelic rebellion. I can easily believe this after piecing together the few inferences in Scripture about conditions prior to Genesis Chapter 1.
2. The earth was somehow devastated—reduced to chaos when God rounded up Satan and his cohorts and brought them to judgment.

Creating, or bringing something into existence out of nothing, is used in Genesis 1:1, where it refers to the original act of creation, and again in Genesis 1:21, where the creation of subhuman creatures is mentioned, and in Genesis 1:27, where the creation of man is described.

So it seems to have been the restoration of a planet that was in a state of chaos. This condition "without form and void" doesn't mean "undeveloped," but rather something which is the result of catastrophe.

This is sometimes called the "gap theory" because of the vast amount of time which must have elapsed between Genesis 1:1 and Genesis 1:2. Dr. Barnhouse calls it "The Great Interval."

He says, "If a perfect God should create a very imperfect world, chaotic, waste, and desolate, a wreck and a ruin, it would be a violation of one of the great spiritual principles stated by the Holy Spirit Himself: 'A fountain cannot send forth sweet water and bitter'"(James 3:11).

After the reconstruction of this earth that had been turned into chaos, God created man. Now man has center stage.

God's Man from Tarsus

Jesus was playing in the streets of Nazareth and Peter was fishing by the sea shore at Bethsaida when Paul was born in Tarsus.

Tarsus was a port of a half million inhabitants, the capital of the Roman province of Cilicia, and described by Paul himself as "No mean city"—that is, no little, insignificant village. It was one of the three great university centers of the ancient world, a city of great commercial activity as well.

Though Tarsus had a large Jewish population who had their own synagogue, it was mainly a heathen city, full of temples to Greek and Roman deities.

The city of Tarsus must have early introduced the young Paul to that diversity of gifts which later gave such trouble at Corinth; for he would have been brought into contact with men and women of different races, colors, and languages. But Paul was brought up in a strict home.

His father was a Pharisee. Yet he had acquired Roman citizenship, which he consequently passed on to his son, when he named Saul, after the first king of Israel from his own tribe of Benjamin.

It is important for us to notice that from the very beginning of his life, Paul's interests were centered in spiritual things.

Few people, if any, have had Paul's particular endowments. In due time, Paul became a rabbi and a member of the Jewish Sanhedrin, the supreme religious authority of his people. He was a zealous Pharisee, a "tell-me-anything more-to-do-and I'll-do-it" Pharisee. He felt if he could just try hard enough he could earn his salvation.

The simple fact is that Paul did not achieve satisfaction by his persecuting of Christians. Perhaps already there was a strong feeling that a sect which produced a Stephen and other such martyrs could not be so far from right. He was soon to find out.

Paul lived a long time ago. How is it that we know so much about him, his ideals, and his thoughts?

The answer is two-fold.

I. Paul attracted the friendship of a very intelligent and devoted Gentile doctor, Luke, by name. Dr. Luke accompanied him on his travels and seems to have kept a diary.

The two probably met at Troas, probably because of Paul's need for medical care. If Dr. Luke dealt medically with Paul, Paul dealt spiritually with Luke.

From Luke and his carefully researched and written account, we gain an insight into the mind of the great Apostle to the Gentiles.

After his remarkable conversion, Paul spent his whole energies and efforts, not simply in converting individuals, but in establishing Christian "cells" in the lands which fringed the Mediterranean—the cities of Asia, Greece, and Macedonia.

II. It is not only from Luke, however, that we gain an insight into the mind of this great soul, but also through Paul's letters to those Christian communities—and in some cases to individuals—we learn to know more about him than about any other person of those long ago days.

Though Paul founded churches in the great pagan cities, he obviously could not be with all of them at the same time. Unfortunately, no sooner did he leave one city than trouble would develop and he was requested to return, or, if he couldn't come in person, at least to give advice. So we have his epistles or letters, which reveal the man Paul in a way that nothing else could.

His letters were often dashed off hurriedly and sent on their way to deal with a pressing situation and to give practical advice. As he dictates to his secretary and walks nervously around the room, he throws out his sentences in rapid succession—thoughts coming into his mind faster than he can express them, faster than the writer can take them down. In his excitement he sometimes forgets the rules of Greek grammar and leaves sentences unfinished. Or he piles words upon words until they become so top-heavy they almost fall. Sometimes he piles one parenthesis on top of another.

Into these letters he empties himself and talks frankly and freely of his own experiences and often of his prejudices.

No doubt at times the harshness of his letters caused him some misgivings. At times he would probably have recalled a letter already on its way. But he was forced to wait anxiously for weeks or months for a response.

Through his entire career Paul had to "fight a good fight" against the corruption of paganism, the antagonism of the Jews, and the intolerance of Christians whose opinions differed from his.

When the leaders in Jerusalem were forced by the results Paul had achieved to acknowledge him as a true missionary of Christ, they did so with reluctance and reservations.

Without the friendship, loyalty, and affection of his Gentile converts—former pagans and heathen—he would have had few to cheer him in times of discouragement or to support him in his efforts.

When, about the year A.D. 66, the news came to Tarsus that Paul had been executed by Nero, we can imagine the talk that went on among the old-timers who had known him in his youth. "Too bad, isn't it? I remember him well: a brilliant young fellow, but queer! He had every chance of making something of himself, but he threw it away!"

Ah, yes, Tarsus. Its people would have been astonished if they had been told that its chief claim to fame was the fact that this man, Paul, who had turned away from the faith of his fathers to follow Jesus, of Nazareth, was born there.

Divine Love Expressed

There is an old legend which states that God called the hosts of heaven together for a conference.

Seated upon His great white throne, He pointed to the earth and directed the attention of the heavenly hosts to the sins of the world—the transgressions, the iniquities, the disobedience of men—in words torn from His very heart.

Out of the emotions of His very soul, He spoke:

"In spite of their shortcomings, I love them. My bowels of mercy and compassion are kindled toward them. They are ungrateful children, disobedient offspring. The tale of their iniquities rises to the very heavens, yet do I love them with an everlasting love and with the cords of mercy would I draw them."

But how? The law must be satisfied; justice must be met. Judgment must find its victim.

"Who will go and tell them of my love, satisfy my law, pay the penalty for their sins, that I might be just and yet justify those who will hear and heed?"

The heavens grew silent. The angels bowed their heads in gloomy thought. The saints stood abashed in quandary of mind. Suddenly there stepped out from the ranks of the angelic host the mighty archangel, Gabriel. Doffing his sword and his trumpet, he prostrated himself before God.

"Lord of heaven and earth!" he said, "Thou hast entrusted me with the leadership of all Thy mighty armies. I have done my best and have tried not to fail Thee. Wilt Thou entrust me with this task?"

God smiled and shook His head: "Nay, Gabriel, thou art the strength of my right hand. No task in heaven, nor on earth is there with which I would not entrust thee, but this is beyond any angel. Someone else must do the required work."

Again stillness reigned over the expanse of Glory. It was broken by the steps of one of the saints. Tall, stately, bearded, his face shining with an unearthly light, he knelt before God.

"Lord," he said, "When I was upon earth, Thou didst call me out from among my brethren. Thou didst entrust me with the commandership of Thy redeemed people. With a mighty hand and outstretched arm, in miraculous, wondrous fashion, Thou didst cause me to lead them out of their galling bondage, almost into the wideness of Thy Promised Land. Let me go back to the earth. Let me tell them the story of Thy love; let my life satisfy the requirements of Thy law."

The Lord's face grew sad and somewhat stern. "Nay, Moses, even thou art not good enough. Someone has to pay for the sin thou didst commit in slaying that Egyptian. Someone has to pay for the sin thou didst commit in striking the rock instead of speaking to it, as I told thee to do. No, Moses, the weight and burden of thy sins is still heavy upon my heart, and still recorded in the records of heaven. They, too, can be washed away only by the blood of some mighty victim."

Suddenly, from the very throne of Glory there came forth a stately figure, outshining the sun in its noon-day splendor. It was Jesus.

Removing the crown of glory from His head and laying aside the robes of majesty from His back, He unloosed the shoes of authority from off His feet and knelt before the Father.

"Father," He pled, "Thou didst use me in the creation of those children of Thine. I, too, have loved them and yearned over them. There is but one more thing I can do for them. Let me go down amongst them. Let me reveal to them Thy love. Let me bear their sins in my own body."

God stooped from His throne, lifted His Son, clasped Him to His breast, and said:

"Go, Thou star of the morning. Let that be Thy mission. Fulfill that which from the beginning of eternity we knew would have to come to pass. Let Thy royal blood expiate the sins of a world."

As the lightning flashes from the east to the west, so Jesus left His glory-circled home in heaven and sped down to the earth. He was born of a virgin in Bethlehem's stable. He grew to manhood in the silent years of Nazareth broken only by His visit to His Father's house at His confirmation.

In the vigor of His manhood, He submitted to the baptism of John. For three years He walked up and down the length and breadth of Palestine—preaching, teaching, healing, working miracles.

He toiled as no man ever toiled; spoke as no man ever spoke; suffered as no man ever suffered. Yet His own received Him not, but cruelly turned their backs on Him. They mocked Him, tortured Him, and nailed Him to the cross. But having accomplished what the Father sent Him to do, He uttered those triumphant words, "It is finished!"

Joseph's sepulcher entombed His lifeless body.

On the third day God raised Him from the dead. For forty days He walked and talked with His disciples. Then He ascended to glory. Now He is seated at the right hand of the Father.

Some day He is coming again to receive His redeemed children unto Himself.

Jesus. Take Him and live! Refuse Him and die.

How Can I Be Sure that God Loves Me?

Here in the majestic train of Old Testament prophecies and in the marvels of New Testament fulfillment concerning the Savior's birth, life, death, and resurrection, we have the most awe-inspiring, faith-instilling truth of all history.

Go back with me to that tragic day when the gates of Paradise were to swing closed upon the outcast parents of the race. Hardly had sin entered the world when a Redeemer was promised. He would be human, because He was the woman's seed, yet divine because He was to perform the superhuman task of destroying sin.

Ages roll on and to Abraham and the Hebrew nation is given the promise that in his seed "all the nations of the earth shall be blessed." Of Abraham's descendants, Jacob and his son Judah are chosen. Centuries are heaped upon centuries, and David is told that the promised Deliverer will be of his royal house and lineage.

The prophet Micah sees Bethlehem as the birthplace of the Messiah. Isaiah speaks of the virgin mother.

Even more sharply does prophecy set before us the great chapters of His world-moving career. Although He will heal the sick and prove Himself the Friend of friends, the Preacher of righteousness, He will be despised and rejected.

Wicked men will take Him captive. He is to be numbered with criminals, His hands and feet and side pierced. He will die a felon's death, and, strangely, instead of an obscure burial in a potter's field, His body is to repose in a rich man's tomb.

Yet, marvel of marvels, He cannot be held in the grip of death. After sinful men had done the worst they could do, He is raised from the dead. He is to ascend on high and be seated at the right hand of God the Father. He will maintain His kingdom and power, and He will strengthen His church for its victorious life through all ages to come.

If Christ so mightily proved His power that He changed the world, and we date our calendar from His birth, shall we not gain strength from the fact that, if every prophecy concerning the past has been fulfilled, every prediction of the future will also be verified?

Although far more has been written about Jesus and His work than about any other figure in history; although marvelous tributes have been paid to His memory in masterpieces of art and architecture, music, and literature, Christ is still the center in a controversy of heated debate. If you cannot explain Christ, you can feel His abiding presence and be sure of His salvation, now and always, because He loves you.

Hallelujah! The Lord Reigneth

The Book of Revelation is an unusual book. Its message is one of victory for the people of God.

You surely must know the historical background of this book. It is one of blood and smoke and martyrdom and intense persecution for God's people.

Here you have the Rome of the Caesars and the Church of the Galilean locked in a death struggle. You have the mailed fist of Nero and Domitian smashing the hopes and dreams of the saints. Everything great and powerful is on the side of Rome.

Here you have, in the words of an Old Testament psalmist, "the kings of the earth taking counsel together against the Lord and His anointed, saying 'let us break their bands asunder, and cast away their cord from us.'"

Here you have the second Babylon, mother of all the abominations of the earth, drunk with the blood of the friends of Jesus, laughing to see the poor, pathetic body of Christ being crushed and mangled and battered out of existence.

That is the background when this man, John, takes up his pen to write, and you and I look over his shoulder, wondering what his message is going to be.

What can he say? What can it be but a lament or an obituary? "The battle is lost; our cause is ruined. The only thing for us to do now is to surrender." Is that what we see him writing? No, a thousand times no! With a defiant and triumphant shout he writes, "Hallelujah! Babylon is fallen, is fallen!"

What made the man write like that? It was because in the background, back of Caesar and all his pomp and pride, John had seen something that would spell the doom of Caesar and of Rome and all others of might and spite like Caesar. He saw a throne set up above the earth and on that throne the Lord God Omnipotent reigning in power!

God's people are on the winning side. We are often inclined to be pessimistic about the future of Christianity. Sometimes we seem to be losing the fight. What will be the final issue in this warfare between good and evil?

To anyone who is really sure of God and His power, it is no longer a wavering question. Anyone who has seen what John saw must know that evil is done for—*already*!

It doesn't look like that when we look at the international scene, at our literature, our morals, our outright siding with things that are wrong.

But remember that God is on the throne; therefore, sin and Satan and evil are doomed!

Hallelujah! The Lord God Omnipotent reigneth!

"It Is the Lord!"

> "Therefore that disciple whom Jesus loved saith unto Peter, It is the Lord" (John 21:7).

"It is the Lord!" These four single syllable words reveal one of the most dramatic statements in history.

"It is the Lord!" This demonstrates recognition of the One who was dead, but is now alive!

These words were uttered by the apostle who has been designated as "John the Beloved." The New Testament man of love was the first to identify the risen Christ on the shores of Galilee.

The subject of recognition after death is something that comes close to home to each of us. Who among us has not asked, "Will we know our loved ones in eternity?"

Jesus Christ, the Eternal Son of God, had been dead and buried. Only a handful of misguided people, infidels and fanatics, have ever denied this fact.

There are no grounds for doubting the New Testament record and the Old Testament prophecies which relate to our Lord's death.

I. Christ had predicted both His death and resurrection
John 2:18-19; John 10:17-18; Luke 9:22; Mark 9:9; Matt. 16:21.

II. He departed this body by His own power, knowing also that He could take His body back again.
The Jews didn't actually kill Jesus or deprive Him of His life, for He surrendered Himself by His own will—"Father, into Thy hands I commend my spirit."

III. The resurrection of Christ is also an historical fact.
It is supported by many infallible proofs.

Of all the miracles recorded in the Bible, it is the greatest. Those three young people: Jarius' daughter (Mark 5:43), the widow's son (Luke 7:15), and Lazarus (John 11:44) died and were raised to die again another day.

With Jesus it was different! Theirs was resuscitation; Christ's was a resurrection!

The spiritual power of the Church is derived from the living Christ. The Christian's hope of eternal life would be a vain delusion if Christ had not risen; but Jesus *did* rise!

Christ was seen of men and women fourteen times after the garden tomb was vacated on the first Easter morning. What more evidence do we need?

There was Mary Magdalene. It was the Lord whom Mary Magdalene saw on the first day of the week when she found the stone rolled away. The empty tomb was mute evidence that Jesus had risen, but somehow the fact did not register in her consciousness. Her first thought was the body had been stolen.

After hearing the angelic messenger, she turned and "saw Jesus standing, and knew not that it was Jesus," that is, until He spoke words of comfort and assurance. It was a dramatic scene. He said, "Mary." She said "Master."

It was the Lord who revealed Himself to the two Mary's, apparently first to one, and later to both (Matt.28:1-10).

It was the Lord who privately gave an interview to Peter on a sacred occasion alluded to twice (Luke 24:34; I Cor. 15:5).

It was the Lord who walked and talked with the couple on the Road to Emmaus and was recognized in the breaking of bread, (Luke 24:15-31).

It was the Lord who appeared to the ten disciples in the Upper Room when Thomas was absent, an event which some chronologists place immediately after the appearance on the shores of Galilee when the fish-catching miracle took place (John 20:19-24; 21:1-24).

Then follows appearances to the eleven on three separate occasions—again in the Upper Room with Thomas present, then later in the same place assembled together with them (Acts 1:4) and on the mountain from which He ascended into heaven (Matt 28:16-20; Acts 1:9).

It was the Lord who appeared to the five hundred at one time and to the apostle James alone (I Cor. 15:6-7).

All these appearances took place prior to the ascension, but did not terminate His presenting Himself to the gaze of others.

It was the Lord who appeared to Stephen as he preached to the Jews and called them "Ye stiff-necked and uncircumcised in heart and ears. Ye do always resist the Holy Ghost . . ." Stephen's hearers snarled at him like wolves about to make the kill. Knowing that His servant was about to leave this world by the way of a violent death, the Lord made a special appearance.

It was the Lord who appeared to Saul on the Road to Damascus. The persecutor heard the voice and recognized the Speaker. He never forgot the experience. Soon he became an apostle. St. Paul's testimony to the resurrection of Christ is one of the strongest in the Scriptures.

Paul longed to know the power of Christ's resurrection. He argued that if Christ be not risen, we who are His shall not rise from the dead, but are of all men most miserable (I Cor. 15:17-19).

It was the Lord who appeared to John the Revelator as he lingered, possibly in chains, a prisoner and exile on the Island of Patmos, a bleak rock in the Agean Sea (Rev. 1:4-20).

II. Seven-fold proof of the resurrection
In addition, there are seven lines of evidence which, considered together, comprise an overwhelming argument that cannot be successfully contradicted.

A. Christ's own life—His birth, teachings, miracles, and His very character necessitated that He come forth from the grave.
B. The empty grave—carefully guarded, closed by a huge stone and sealed, yet vacated. The cloths that

were wrapped about His body and head were left undisturbed by His emerging from the tomb.
C. The transformed disciples—formerly weak and wavering in faith, doubters; then after the resurrection and after Pentecost, every one of them fearless in the face of death at the hands of Jews and infidels. These men preached the resurrection because they were absolutely convinced.
D. The human witnesses—hundreds of them, sometimes singly, other times in groups.
E. The early church—founded by Christ through His own words and the testimony of convinced and consecrated disciples. It has grown and increased in strength so that today its nominal members aggregate over four hundred million.
F. The skeptical Jew, prejudiced Pharisee and persecutor of the Christians—Saul of Tarsus. The risen Christ took St. Paul in hand and revealed Himself to this fanatical unbeliever. From then on, there was no greater preacher of Christ's resurrection.
G. The complete gospel record—contained in the New Testament, written after the events took place and never successfully discredited by an unbeliever or any other enemy. Historically, it takes its place as the purest, cleanest history ever written.

Christ's resurrection was consistent with the prophetical Scriptures. "He was buried, and rose the third day, according to the Scriptures."

Christ's resurrection was consistent with His personal predictions and promises.

Christ's resurrection was consistent with the demands of His holiness, which also embraces His veracity and honesty. Had He not risen again, His word would have been discredited.

Christ's resurrection was consistent with His divine power

to perform supernatural deeds, the result of His supernatural origin and being.

The miracles He performed were demonstrations of His deity, but the most amazing of all was this one in which, after being dead and buried, He made Himself to live again amongst men.

"Lord, Teach Us to Pray"
Luke 11:1

Suppose you were one of the mythical men from Mars on a visit to this planet. On this first day of the week you would see multitudes of human beings making their way to buildings which they call churches. There they would bow their heads while a man or woman stood in front of them and talked to a Being whom he called God, but whom you could not see. Perhaps your first reaction would be to say that such doings were bewildering to say the least.

At night you would see still more people kneeling beside their beds and saying words to that invisible Somebody. When you asked what they were doing, you were told that they were praying.

Then you learned that this practice had been going on day in and day out since the dawn of history; that people had risked their lives for the right to pray; that they had sacrificed untold labor and money to build beautiful places in which to pray.

As you pondered all this, wouldn't you become deeply curious about the universal and persistent practice of prayer? Surely you would feel that there must be something to this business of praying which has kept it going through the ages.

Now suppose you could be carried back, as if by magic, across the centuries to a land where the people were much given to prayer. Social and political leaders would make long prayers in public. Yet their praying didn't make much difference in their lives. Then in the midst of them you noticed a young man who seemed to feel that the God to whom He prayed was as near to Him as the man upstairs.

You would see this young man stop and talk to His God beside the road and then go on, filled with a new spirit and power. Or He might stand in front of a hostile crowd or on the deck of a storm-tossed ship and talk to an Invisible Being whom He called "Father" and immediately results became visible, changing situations. After watching this Man and the results of His prayers day after day, you would probably go to Him and say, "Teach me to pray?"

That's what the disciples of Jesus did more than 2000 years ago. They saw Jesus use prayer so naturally and effectively that they longed to learn His secret.

I wonder if we do not feel as the disciples felt. The impulse to pray is as natural as breathing. Perhaps most of us say our prayers, some more regularly than others. But are we making full and satisfying use of prayer? How real are the prayers we pray and the answers we receive?

When the disciples said to Jesus, "Teach us to pray," they probably wanted Him to teach them a prayer which they could repeat, for that is what the rabbis were accustomed to do for their pupils. And Jesus *did* give them a model prayer. We call it the Lord's Prayer.

But the Master was not content to have them merely learn a model prayer. He gave other directions for prayer which are scattered throughout the gospels. So when we seek to learn from Jesus how to pray, we must take into account His whole teaching on that subject.

We usually assume that the crux of the matter is "Does God give us what we ask for?" But before asking God for what *we* want, we must make sure we give Him what *He* wants of us.

In our Lord's model prayer, we first look at God, saying, "Our Father which art in heaven, hallowed be Thy name." Then we're taught to say, "Thy kingdom come. Thy will be done on earth as it is in heaven."

Of what do you think when you repeat those words? When we pray for His will to be done, we must start with ourselves. "Thy kingdom come *in me*. Thy will be done *in me*."

Such a prayer is really an offering rather than a petition. God's kingdom is waiting to come into us whenever we surrender our wills and give God our hearts.

Do we really want God's will to be done in us even if it means giving up some pleasing but pernicious habit or humbling ourselves to forgive another?

Having surrendered our will to God's, we are ready for the next step in prayer, our petitions. But we want so many things! Jesus taught us to begin by asking for the *essentials of life*, "our daily bread." When we ask for our daily bread, we are asking for enough to live on while we are seeking to do His will.

Maybe some of us ask for too much and others fail to ask for as much as we should. When we bring our desires to God we begin to see what is right to ask for.

Jesus said, "Whatsoever ye shall ask in my name, that will I do." This requirement limits our requests. What can we ask for in Christ's name?

Can I pray for health? Yes, if I desire strength of body not merely for my own selfish indulgence, but rather to serve God. Can I pray for success in my business engagements? Yes, providing the purpose of my business is to further Christ's kingdom interests.

When we pray in Christ's name, we are kept from asking for unworthy or selfish things. But we also are led to ask for things which we had not thought of in our selfishness. We are led to think of others. We realize that there is one whom we have wronged and we go on to pray, "Forgive us our trespasses."

Then our horizon lifts and we look ahead to our tomorrows. We pray, "Lord, lead us not into temptation but deliver us from evil." If we wish God to forgive us, then we must not loiter around the old temptations until we fail again.

Jesus taught us to pray, not only for the essential bread to see us through the day, but also for forgiveness of the past and the safeguarding of our tomorrows.

While the model prayer which our Lord taught us ends with these brief petitions, His teaching *about* prayer goes further. After

Jesus has finished giving us this model, He tells us to *pray without ceasing.*

We are to ask persistently, to seek sincerely, and to knock expectantly. We are to persevere in praying as did the importunate friend at midnight, asking for food for a friend who had come to visit him.

Prayer, as Jesus taught us, becomes a continuing channel of passionate and loving intercession. Prayer, inspired by love and tested by the spirit of Christ, has no limit to its range and power.

Sir George Adam Smith once said that we never discover the power of prayer until our prayers look up to God like wounded animals with great, large, round eyes of pain.

Tennyson wrote:

> "More things are wrought by prayer
> Than this world dreams of."

How true. But if we are to receive answers to our prayers, we must remember that prayer is never designed to alter God's will, but to ascertain it.

The Blessing of the Gospel
Rom. 15:29

It was the dream of Paul's life to see Rome—not only to see it, but to win it to Christ. Now the hour had come for him to assault the pagan powers at the headquarters and to bring Christ and His blessed gospel to Caesar's domain.

Here was Rome, the metropolis of the world, proud and regal, sitting on her seven hills, ruling with an iron rod, and shaking the earth with the marching of her invincible armies.

Here, on the other side was this little, frail-looking Jew, with nothing to commend him—no credentials, no references nor testimonials from important people—nothing but what he called his gospel.

"I am sure . . . ." See how he loads his language, how he piles the words up, one on top of the other, until the sentence becomes toy-heavy and begins to stagger with the weight of its truth. "I am sure . . . ."

Let's take each of the four items separately, beginning with the last.

1. "I am coming to you with Christ." Jesus passed across a narrow corner of an obscure subject land, and there He left His footprints so deep the ages have not obliterated them.
   Paul is coming with Christ, not a new philosophy of life, not even a new political theory. Rome was often rent with strife, hatred, and division.
   But Paul was offering the one and only remedy for Rome's wickedness.
   Paul is coming with Christ, not a new interpretation of religion. He didn't say, "I am coming to you with Christianity."
2. "I am coming to you with the Gospel of Christ." "Gospel" means "good news." Jesus came! He died! He is alive! He offers forgiveness for sin and a heaven for His followers!
3. The blessing of the Gospel—it gives hope to the hopeless, help to the helpless, and love to the loveless.
4. "The fullness of the blessing of the Gospel." The blessings of the gospel extend to every area of life.

Years ago a hurricane destroyed a little church on the coast of England. The people were not able to get the money needed to replace the building, so they made provisions to worship elsewhere.

One day a representative of the British Admiralty called on the minister to ask when the church, with its steeple, would be rebuilt. He was told of the situation—a lack of money.

The government representative said, "Since that is so, we will rebuild it for you because that spire is on all our navigation charts and our ships all steer their courses by it."

The story is told of a lost child in a big city. An officer picked the child up and started driving around to find the child's home. Finally, the child said, "Mister, if you'll take me to my church, I can find the way home."

That's really the purpose of the gospel—to show us the way home.

When It Pays to Be Poor
Matt. 5:3

The first Beautitude arouses curiosity in the modern mind. The word "poor" arouses curiosity because most of us are trying to get rich, not poor.

Several translations in modern speech use the word "happy" in place of "blessed." This translation adds confusion to complicity. How can one harmonize the poor and the happy?

The American idea of happiness is to own a nice home, a large TV set, a new Cadillac, fine furniture, and plenty of food and clothing, a big bank account and insurance on the whole family. That is happiness according the American way of thinking.

Christ's thinking, acting, and living were not tainted by the American Way. Judged by our standards, Jesus was a failure in every way. Surely our Lord would term the American way a lazy, soft, careless, and aimless way.

The characteristic of our age seems to be to get all that is coming to you and a little bit more. Assert yourself. Be aggressive. Be self-sufficient. Be the perfect example of the self-made man.

But Jesus taught just the opposite. He gives us in the third Beautitude a definition of humility, which is the strength of the perfect life.

All of Jesus' teachings are a direct thrust at the heart of false pride.

1. The poor in spirit have a feeling of unworthiness. They feel unworthy of the great salvation and all the blessings God has provided for them.
2. The poor in spirit feel their utter dependence upon God.

When they need counsel, they ask God in child-like faith for it. Then they receive and accept it.

When they need strength, they go to God for it. Then they can say with Paul, "I can do all things through Christ which strengtheneth me" (Phil.4:13).

How to Make Life worth Living

Jesus said, "I am come that they might have life, and that they might have it more abundantly" (John 10:10).

It is no prosaic or dull existence that Christ offers to man. It is a vigorous, victorious and enduring life, one which maintains a correspondence, not merely with the physical and material—the here and now—but one which reaches out to correspond with the environment of Eternity.

We all know that it is not the many, but the few, who achieve a full, rich, happy, outreaching life. We are too easily satisfied with life's second best.

Not one of us has achieved more that a fraction of his capacity for a full, rich, satisfying life. The greatest of us reach only 15-20 percent of our capabilities. What about the rest of us? God wants us to live life to the full.

The skeptic Voltaire said we ought to try to hold it fast in our minds: "Most men died without having lived."

While Jesus walked and talked with men and ministered to their infirmities, He always had windows opening out to the infinite. He lived constantly in tune with Heaven. Into a life with such an outlook and uplook He seeks to lift us too.

What an amazing transformation Jesus wrought upon His disciples—these fishermen, tax collectors, peasants—with more than average human failures! Under the spell of Christ, they grew into spiritual giants who have become the inspiration of the ages.

Even so, it is beyond our power to estimate what might be

accomplished in each of us if we would let Christ have His way. Then we could go back to the stubborn personal problem which has defeated us or to that difficulty which looms above our pathway like an impassable barrier, and by the power of Christ within us we would win victory at the very point of former defeat and failure.

We have all seen the miracle whereby Christ lays hold of commonplace human lives and fashions them into courageous, resolute, consecrated personalities so that almost every semblance of their former selves has disappeared.

You and I can enter into that abundant life only as we yield ourselves in complete surrender to Him who is the Lord of life and say with the poet, "Have thine own way, Lord." Then we shall discover this abundant life as we lose ourselves in a cause greater than our own.

We need three things in order to make life really count: (1) a faith to live by, (2) a self fit to live with, and (3) a cause to live for.

The cause of Christ and His kingdom inspired men like St. Paul, St. Francis, Savanorola, Luther, Knox, Wesley, Phillips Brooks, Beecher, and a host of others.

You can live a life that is different or be just an ordinary, mediocre Christian. Your influence will live on.

Someone asked, "When at last the busy world is hushed and the fever of life is over and your work is done, and you are called to stand before Him and give an account of your stewardship, will there be a continuing witness to God's kingdom left in the world as evidence that you have passed this way?"

The God of the Living

> "Jesus answered and said unto them . . . have ye not read that which was spoken unto you by God saying, 'I am the God of Abraham, and the God of Isaac, and the God of Jacob? God is not the God of the dead, but of the living'" (Matt.22:29, 31.32).

The Sadducees of ancient Jerusalem were not without religion of a sort. They had a vague sense of God who once lived in a glorious past. It was only that, for them, God had faded out; He didn't matter any more.

The Sadducees were the wealthy, worldly people of Jerusalem in charge of the Temple business. They were the "old family," the intelligentsia, the priestly aristocracy. They were not the least interested in Jesus from a religious point of view, as were the Pharisees. They would never have condescended to notice Jesus at all had He not become so troublesome.

He had upset their money-tables, interfered with the business of the Temple, and taught the people that God loved Gentiles as well as Jews.

They couldn't have fanatics like that running loose, breaking up furniture, ruining the tourist business, and encouraging equality among the races! So they joined forces with their old enemies, the Pharisees, to embarrass Jesus and to find some way to get rid of Him.

In the Temple one day they brought Him a question, an old question that they had been harping on for generations. There was no resurrection; they *knew* that! Only simple folks believed such a thing. [Dr. Mendell Taylor says that's why they were "sad you see"]. As for people having souls, well, maybe they did, but what difference did it make? This world was the real thing.

So they brought out this old hypothetical question about the woman who had been married seven times. All seven husbands were dead. "Whose wife will she be in the resurrection?" It was a trivial, shallow question, yet what an answer Jesus gave to it! He said, "He is not a God of the dead, but of the living."

This is a basic truth. Our faith in eternal life is based, not on any wishful thinking we may entertain about heaven, nor on any pictures that our finite minds may draw about the future life. Our whole confidence is grounded in the nature and character of God. All our human hopes for the here and for the hereafter are grounded in the fact that "He is not the God of the dead, but of the living."

1. He is the God of a living universe. We cannot treat this

fact lightly. It is a mistake to think of the resurrection of Christ or of our own immortality as something apart from life, without previous pattern and preparation. We are discovering that this creation is far more wonderful than we had ever dreamed; and that running through it all, from atom to star, is the inescapable evidence of Mind and Intelligence, of design and progressive movement toward a goal.

Everything in the universe is alive! We know that now. Nothing is solid or static, inert or dead. We, ourselves, are standing on a star, moving swiftly. Tiny worlds beneath us, miniatures of the larger worlds above, are moving too. The kingdom of nature is made up of an intricate network of invisible, living, moving forces, acting and grouping themselves with an intelligence that is unbelievable.

Everything in the universe is not only moving and living, but related. It all fits together, hangs together in a continuous scheme like the human body, with all its parts related to all other parts. "What does it all mean" asked Dr. Millikan, "after a lifetime of pushing back curtains, only to find more and more curtains? Simply this: that there is in nature a vast interrelatedness and a unity, and beyond, still an amazing mystery."

How easy it is to go up from this amazing design in nature to the higher purpose for which all nature is only a preparation, and to find in the movement of human history the *God of a living purpose!*

Jesus was trying to drum into dull ears back there in the Temple the truth that God was not dead, nor distant, but He is living in human history and working out His purpose in their midst.

These Sadducees should have known from the history of their own people that He was a God of continuing, progressive purpose. Who was Abraham? He was the father of this nation, Israel, through whom God had begun a new redemptive purpose in history, as wide as the world and as indestructible as God Himself.

When you open the Bible, you find that it is not just history;

it is the story of the progressive unfolding of God's purpose in history. It tells us that history has been upset periodically by new light breaking in from God, changing men and through them changing history. As you turn the pages of the Bible and watch the human drama unfold, you begin to see in history what scientists find in nature—the inescapable evidence of a Superior Intelligence working toward a higher purpose than our highest thought.

The whole history of man is summed up in the story of the cross, in the picture of the patient, yet persistent, God striving with the stubborn heart of man, trying to break through his ignorance, sin, and dullness of mind to get His will done.

That is what Jesus was up against at the Temple. He tried to get these dull believers in a dead God—who had once spoken to Abraham and Moses and then closed the book—to see that God is the God of the living.

2. God's purpose cannot be defeated. How often men have thought that Christ was finished, His cause was done for. But, behold, He is alive again! Just as they could not kill the life in Him, neither can men kill the causes in which His spirit lives. What can you do with a force like that? The empty grave in Palestine is the open mouth of God calling to all the centuries, "Know ye not that you can never defeat God's eternal purpose?" You may sometimes seem to defeat it, but after you have done your worst, it will still be there, judging you as deathless as life itself.

A Christian philosopher said he wished people would stop trying to prove the future life as if our faith depended on mathematical proof. He said, "When God wants to carry a point with His children He plants it deeper than the mind, in the instinct." That is why we can never really disbelieve in the fact of our immortality. We try hard enough, as did the Sadducees. We have a lot of questions about it, as did the Sadducees, and often for the same reason.

But, try as we will, we cannot put it out of our minds, for it is planted, not in the mind, but deeper, in the instinct. He is not a God of the dead, but of the living. If it all ends in a hole in the ground, then nothing makes sense, and life is left pointless and meaningless. We cannot believe that we spend a life-time getting ready for something, and when we get there—nothing!

Or we spend years in developing a mind; then when it is ready for great achievement, it's snuffed out!

Or we walk with God through the years while He builds in us a great character, and then when it is bright enough to shine a light to others, it is blown out like a candle in the night. We must believe better of God than that.

Bulwar said, "I cannot believe that earth is man's real abiding place; that our life is cast up by the ocean of eternity to float a moment upon its waves, and then sink into nothingness; else why is it that the glorious aspirations which leap like winged angels from the temple of our heart are forever wandering about unsatisfied? . . . We are born for a higher destiny than that of earth . . . . there is a realm where the rainbow never fades, where the stars will be spread before us like islands that slumber on the ocean: and where these beings that pass before us like shadows in the night will stay in our presence forever."

So we believe that God, the God of the living, has put us here to live in an exciting, living universe, to co-operate with an eternal, undying purpose. And because He lives, all the doors are open, even this: because He lives, we too shall live *for* Him and *with* Him forever.

CHAPTER 5

Glimpses into Truth

Karl Marx said that society was the seat of the conflicts that destroy us. Kierkegaard said it was in man's soul. Modern psychology has voted for Kierkegaard.

The peace of God that surpasses human understanding is offered by Jesus. It is neither the peace of withdrawal from conflict, nor of flight from the battle, nor of surrender to the enemy. It is the peace of inner security. It is a calmness of soul in the midst of turmoil

One harsh word from a friend may give greater pain than a flood of abusive words from an enemy.

Our dead loved ones who belonged to the Lord Jesus are not behind us now, but before us. And, though it may seem a long time since we left them back there at the parting, the passing years are not taking us farther from them but closer to them.

Sin is not just a word. It is everything that is repulsive to God. Sin is a word we use to describe a mode of living that is in rebellion to Almighty God.

Many of us have trouble believing that God has done what He has, that Christ is who He is, and that He can do what He says He can do.

To realize that God is only a prayer away is one of the most important discoveries we can make.

Jesus left a throne for a manger that He might fill the mansions of heaven with redeemed citizens.

Joy is that elusive thing that some people try to buy with money, generate at a party, or look for in a bottle, but never find because they are searching in the wrong places.

Robert L. Stevenson said that the appearance of a good man is "as though another candle had been lighted."

People who talk about the "good old days" didn't think they were good days when they were living through them.

We can't always take credit for our successes; neither should we blame someone else for our failures.

This universe is a vast tinderbox and God has hidden the matches. Now that man has found the matches, he knows what could happen, and he stands shivering with fear.

A problem is a set of circumstances which threatens our well being. Circumstances are people and things. So solving our problems means getting people and things the way we want them.

When we would utter our deepest thought about life and what it means, about God and what He is, one word leaps to our lips—love.

Existence is what we find; life is what we make of it.

Jesus devoted Himself to meeting the needs of the people of His day. He is still meeting our needs today.

Thousands of people—especially young people—want nothing to do with organized religion. Yet many of them are sincerely seeking for something to fill what H.G. Wells called "the God-shaped emptiness" in their lives.

We do not need to be afraid of life. Our hearts are sometimes very frail and faith falters. The road is sometimes steep and lonely. But we have a wonderful God. As St. Paul puts it, "Who can separate us from the love of God?"

Starting as we all do with families and comparatively easy demands, we run sooner or later into some situation—difficult, perilous, or tragic—that requires of us more power than life ever asked of us before, and that demand becomes critical.

Life need not defeat us, however. We need not crack up. Even in the worst times, we need not merely to be resigned to bear our troubles. We need to take them to the Lord.

Get out an old photograph of yourself at 16, 18, or 20. Look into your youthful eyes and ask yourself some questions:
Have I lost some of my dreams?
Are my ideals as high now as they were then?
Am I as committed now?
Are my tastes more wholesome than ever?
Can I still commit my most serious problems to God?
What have I learned?
Where do I go from here?

As one who over the years has tried to apply the lessons of history to modern problems, I am convinced that unless and until we are able to change the basic characteristics of human nature, the old virtues and values are still the most pertinent and perhaps even the most vital for our survival.

Dr. Louis H. Evans said, "We boast on Sunday that we are

the children of God, yet we live the rest of the week as though we were orphans."

If you have a little God you will have big problems. If you have a big God you will have little problems.

It is not so much what we do for God that counts as it is what we let Him do through us.

One man said, "I've got problems. I live with a problem. I am a problem."

God does not ask about our ability or inability, but rather our availability.

An old scholar who was dying said to his friends, "Do you realize that in an hour or two I will know the answers for which we have been searching all our lives?"

Walter Lippmann said:

> "Whatever is poor wants to be rich;
> whatever is slow wants to be fast;
> whatever is small wants to be large;
> whatever IS anything wants to be MORE SO."

God has a wonderful plan for you. You cannot fail to be successful if you allow Him to do for you, in you, and with you what He has in mind.

It is the person who is living a life that is broad enough and good enough to last forever who expects that it will.

If all our hurry and worry only gets us that much faster to the cemetery, why should we permit them?

If you practice the presence of God in this life, you can never know separation from Him.

Jesus is preparing a mansion only for those who want one.

Be careful what you go after in life. The chances are that you'll get it. But it may be all you get.

Man needs to have something to live for, someone to love, some purpose in life, something to which he can give himself in dedication.

The church today has a great message from a great God for a needy people.

If you want to be miserable, think always of yourself—what you like, what you want, what respect people ought to pay to you, and what people think about you.

Dorothy Thompson, noted world observer, wrote: "We are in a new Dark Ages. Civilization has already capitulated to barbarism by default of its own standards."

Walter Lippman wrote: "No mariner has ever entered upon a more uncharted sea than the human being born in our Today.
"Never were roads wilder, nor sign posts fewer. Our ancestors knew their way from birth through death into eternity, but we're puzzled about day after tomorrow."

Life is like climbing a mountain. You never get there. There is always a higher peak up ahead.

There are two kinds of disappointed people. There are those who are disappointed because they *do not* get what they want and those who are disappointed because they *do* get what they want.

Everyone you meet is probably waging a desperate battle if you only knew it.

Some people are more afraid to live than to die. That's why they take their own lives.

The greatest need of Christians today is to have the courage to live the Christian faith.

God takes us off our own hands and gives us back to ourselves as new creatures.

If people do not really believe we have found something that is very important to us, why should they want it?

The most sensitive nerve in a man's body is his pocketbook.
The use of money reveals character.
The love of money turns good men into bad.
Money does strange things to people; it can blot out every thought of God. And it can harden hearts and dwarf souls.

Joy is the identifiable mark of a Christian. If our loved ones don't see joy in our lives, there's something wrong.
Joy is the ecstasy of God, the outer expression of an inner experience of grace.

It is detrimental to true religion when we exalt Christ in our form of worship and then disgrace Him in our manner of living.

Some years ago an economist said, "America is dangling at the end of a rope of sand." He was speaking of our economic structure. But he could have made this statement apply to our social, moral, even our religious life.

A new day would dawn, a new grace and glory would come in the church if all her people stopped doing things for themselves and did them for God.

The church is in less danger from active devils than from inactive members.

Salvation is not some vague or remote thing that has to do with another world. It is the infusion of life and power into all the concerns and affairs of this world.

How a person can look out on our lovely world day after day, eat three good meals a day, live for seventy years, and not find any time to think of his relationship to God and his need of God is a mystery. Yet there are those who do.

Dr. Francis Shaeffer, Christian scholar from Switzerland, said, "This is not an age to be a soft Christian."

Jesus chose His men that He might have a little circle of kindred spirits and that He might write His message upon them.

A miracle, to Jesus, was not a means of increasing His prestige; to help was not a disagreeable duty. He helped because He was interested in all who needed His help.

The nearer a person lives to God, the surer he is of being with Him both here and hereafter.

The day is done. It is time to sail out on that last voyage on that sea where there are no wrecked ships nor the bones of lost mariners—the sea of God's mercy which brings us to the City of Eternal Life.

G. K. Chesterton said, "Whatever else is or is not true, this one thing is certain. Man is not what he was meant to be."

If God and man can enter into fellowship, man must matter to God.

A. J. Gordon said, "Before Pentecost the disciples found it hard to do easy things; after Pentecost they found it easy to do hard things."

If one is going to live forever, why should he worry over three score years and ten?

Is it possible that God, who hates sin, has so created us that we can resist Him and not resist the devil? If one never read more of the Bible than the first chapter of the New Testament, he could see that Christ came to save us *from* our sins.

The gospel is not something for us to come to church to hear. It is something for us to go from the church to tell.

The church of the catacombs has always been stronger than the church of the cathedrals.

We open the windows of our minds and the doors of our wills to God. That is what God's rule means in our lives.

Any movement, religion included, must have devoted followers in order to succeed. Until compromise is replaced by unswerving loyalty, what we profess will have little effect in determining the course we actually pursue.

Science has not so much banished God as it has made substitutes for Him convenient and plentiful.

We cannot live on the spiritual capital inherited from another generation.

The real value of religion depends on how much its believers are willing to risk for it.

Three things characterized the early Christians: They were courageous; they were always cheerful; they were always getting into trouble.

Man is a being for whom God cares and on whom God makes claim for worship and obedience.

Man is not a body and a mind; he is also a spiritual being made in the image of God, capable of worshipping, obeying, and trusting his Maker.

Resolve to be tender with the young, compassionate with the aged, sympathetic with the striving, and tolerant with the weak and those in the wrong. Sometime in your life you will have been all of these.

Eskimo proverb: "May you always have warmth in your igloo, oil in your lamp, and peace in your heart."

No wonder they call Jesus the Savior. Because of the cross we know that our failures are not final, our lives are not futile, and our deaths are not final.

In the cross we find forgiveness, purpose, and rest from the storms of life.

When Jesus came to earth He laid aside His divine glory. Yet it shone through at His angel-heralded birth, at His first miracle at Cana, at His dazzling transfiguration, at His resurrection, and at His ascension.

Three essentials truths: God is completely sovereign; He is infinite in wisdom; and He is perfect in love.

It would be as impossible to read the New Testament and escape the message of brotherhood as it would be to swim the English Channel without getting wet.

Abundant life, eternal life, everlasting life is the message of the New Testament. Abundant life does not mean an abundance of possessions. Nor can life be identified with length of days.

The church is not a collected group of acquaintances. It is not even a gathering of friends. It is a family of God.

Some go so far as to say that the acceptance of the Christian way need not make very much difference in a person's life. St. Paul would have said it makes all the difference in the world.

God watches when every other eye is closed; He guides when every other arm drops helpless.

Watching people, we may be inclined to think that most of them expect to find life ready-made and quite good and happy. But we never *find* life. All we find is the raw material—sometimes rough and not very promising—out of which we have to *make* a life.

The real business of life is not to make a fortune to leave behind, but to grow a character that is good enough to last forever.

With the coming of Jesus a new element entered into the life of humanity, a new law was discovered, a new power was released, a new rhythm of being was revealed.

There is something eternal in our human souls, something deeper than our fears and tears, deeper even than our love.
The more we know of the human spirit, the more we are sure that there is an Eternal Spirit seeking us. The fact that the spiritual life exists in us, that we need God, that we seek God, and that we aspire to know and love God is the most amazing fact in life.

Martin Luther said, "If I were God and the world had treated me as it has treated Him, I would have kicked the whole thing to pieces long ago."

The unholy Christian is a contradiction of everything the Bible teaches.

Even though our civilization, like others before it, finally flickers out, and institutional Christianity with it, the light that Jesus shed centuries ago will shine as brightly as ever for those who seek an escape from the darkness of this world.

CHAPTER 6

Anecdotes

From Pittsburgh comes an amazing story of a 65-year-old widow, with almost a million dollars at her disposal who lived in the worst kind of poverty.

She could have bought her clothing from the most fashionable stores, but she wore rags.

She could have employed servants to help her, but she lived alone in a pretentious mansion.

She could have eaten the best foods, but she was almost starved to death and was so weak from hunger that she could only crawl on hands and knees.

She had $200,000 in uncashed dividend checks and an unused bank account of $65,000; yet she was probably hungrier and more destitute than the poorest person in Pittsburgh.

Arthur Rubinstein was once so depressed that he came close to ending his life. But the belt he planned to use to hang himself broke. He fell to his knees, and when he got up, he was suddenly surrounded by an awareness of the beauty of life all around him.

"I have loved living ever since," he confessed to Barbara Walters in a TV interview.

John Wesley had always thought he was a true Christian until one day his ship was caught in a bad storm in the Atlantic and fear got hold of him.

He noticed that the only people on board who were not afraid were a little group of Moravian missionaries. When the storm abated, Wesley asked one of them, "Were you not afraid?"

"Afraid?" said the Moravian, "why should I be afraid? I know Christ!"

And then looking at Wesley with frankness, he asked, "Do you know Christ?" And Wesley, for the first time in his life, realized that he did not.

Bishop Moore said he grew up in a small town in South Georgia, where he remembered them singing in the Sunday school: "There's a Wideness in God's Mercy like the Wideness of the Sea."

The biggest body of water he'd seen was a small mill pond. He thought that people who live inland should not sing that song. They should go to the sea to appreciate it.

In his duties for the church, he and his wife made a voyage across the ocean and for 35 days saw no land at all. They had almost forgotten what land looked like.

"Then," he said, "a person can stand somewhere on the ship, and even if he doesn't have a good voice or isn't much of a singer, he can sing, 'There's a Wideness in God's Mercy like the Wideness of the Sea.'"

If you have been to the sea, you know.

Dr. A. T. Pierson said on one occasion that he once visited a devout woman who had lost her aged and saintly mother. He was thinking what he might say to offer sympathy, when the woman said, with a smile: "For forty years my dear mother's mind has been in heaven while she lived here on earth."

Charles Darwin visited Tierra del Fuego in 1833 and found its people bestial and crude, almost beyond description.

Thirty-six years later he revisited the island and discovered that these same people lived in an entirely different culture—literate, gentle, and hospitable. They had been changed by the gospel.

In amazement, Darwin sent twenty-five pounds to the London Missionary Society and asked that he be enrolled as an honorary member.

Here were people on this remote savage island who had not only been educated, but they had also been made over into new beings by Christianity.

That's Christian rebirth.

One of the richest gold mines of the west was once the property of a poor prospector. He grew weary in his search and finally laid down his tools only a foot from one of the greatest fortunes on record. He went away a poor man and another man reaped what might have been his.

Captain Eddie Rickenbacker has flirted with death many times and escaped its clutches.

Years ago, when he crashed in an airplane, he was taken to a hospital. Everyone thought he would die. When he didn't die, they told him he would never use his right hand again.

Rickenbacker lay in bed and looked at his hand. He had always been a person of simple, childlike faith. He held his hand up to the greatest Doctor of all, saying, "God, I believe You can heal this hand."

It seemed that God gave him the assurance that the two together would do it.

So Eddie asked the nurse to anchor a glass on a small table. Day after day, week after week he went to work with his fingers, asking God to help him; exercising faith, manhood, character, struggling to get his fingers around that glass.

One day he achieved success. How did he do it? With God's help and by using all the faith and determination he had.

One of the greatest of all American sculptors was Gutson Borglum, who died in 1941. He made the massive likenesses of four U.S. Presidents—Washington, Jefferson, Lincoln, and Theodore Roosevelt—on Mt. Rushmore in the Black Hills of South Dakota.

At one time before he undertook this great task, he worked for about a year on a six-ton block of marble.

A woman who cleaned his studio frequently wondered what that great block of stone was to be. Finally after much toil, the features began to emerge from the stone.

The woman said, "How did Mr. Borglum know that Abraham Lincoln was in that bit of stone?"

God wants to shape us into His image.

Dr. L.A. Banks tells the story of a man getting up in years, who had grown hard, selfish, narrow, and mean as he grew older.

His wife and children had gone out for the evening. Sitting at the table after eating, he dozed.

The doorbell rang. A servant brought him a man's card and his glasses. The man came into the room.

They talked pleasantly. The stranger grew up in the same locality, knew all his family and schoolmates, and a girl he had liked very much and his wife had the same name.

His visitor was a distinguished man of letters, but in the rush he hadn't read his books, a man who had helped the poor.

Leaving, he walked by a mirror—so much like him in the better years; the man left.

He looked at the card. His own name and the words: "I am the man you might have been!"

He awoke from his dream. But what a message!

We are naturally inclined to accept ourselves as we are and to be content with that. So we just "knuckle under" and drift along with the stream.

Do you remember the scene in Dickens' *A Tale of Two Cities* where Sidney Carton, the man with good possibilities, was walking through the lifeless desert of London's streets in the gray twilight of the dawn?

Suddenly he paused, for in front of him was a vision—the vision of a life, his life, crowned with nobility and self-denying usefulness and love. But the vision was only a mocking mirage. A moment, then it was gone.

He climbed to his lonely garret and flung himself down on his neglected bed, and his pillow was wet with his wasted tears.

He had been giving in to his temptations, taking for granted his lapses from trying to be good, too tame to stand up and strike a blow for freedom.

"This is all I have in my power to be," he says, "And for the future, why worry?"

But that is by no means the end of the story. He redeems himself by giving his life to spare the life of another man.

In the depression days of 1929 a man lost his business over night. The shock of it was too much for him at the time.

One evening, at sunset, with one nickel and three pennies in his pocket, this man walked out into a field. He didn't see the glory of a waning day. He didn't feel the cool evening air. All he could see was the misery of his own mind and the hopelessness of his world.

In his hand he held a bottle marked POISON. He raised the bottle to his lips and drank. It burned his lips and throat. He fell to the ground and lost consciousness.

After a while he opened his eyes. He was amazed that he was alive. He lay there in that field, looking up into the heavens. And he began to think about God.

The son of a minister, he was brought up in the church.

He began to pray, "Lord, I tried to kill myself, and I ask Your forgiveness. If you will let me live, I will surrender myself to You completely. I will serve You the rest of my life and do as much for You as I can."

God answered his prayer. Today hundreds of people say he has changed their lives. That day when he went out into the field with the bottle of poison in his hand was not to be the end of his life and influence.

At one time Mahatma Ghandhi looked into the Christian faith. For several Sundays he attended a Christian church.

But he said, "The congregation didn't strike me as being religious at all. They were not an assembly of devout people; they appeared to be worldly-minded people, going to church for recreation and in conformity to custom."

He concluded that there was nothing in Christianity that he didn't already have.

So Ghandhi was lost to the Christian faith, and though he had a far reaching effect on India, he might have had a greater influence for righteousness.

Describing what life was like to him, Tolstoy tells the story of an Oriental explorer who was attacked by a tiger.

Running from the tiger, the explorer came to a dry well and leaped into it. He caught hold of a bush at the top wall of the well and held fast to it.

Looking down toward the bottom of the well, he saw a mad dragon, mouth open, ready to snatch and devour the man as soon as he fell. The man determined to hold on to the shrub as long as possible.

Then he saw two mice, one was black, the other white. They

began to gnaw at the root of the shrub. The man couldn't release his grip to chase them away, so it was a matter of time.

Many of us see life just as hopeless as this. But Jesus came to give us hope and abundant life. He said He came so that we "might have life and have it more abundantly." That means to have a surplus or an over-abundance of something.

A Roman soldier came to Julius Caesar with a request for permission to commit suicide. He was a wretched, miserable, dejected fellow, with no vitality about him.

Caesar looked at him and said, "Man, were you ever really alive?"

When we live with Christ and for Christ, life becomes really worth living.

A miner who had been a drunken reprobate was converted. His fellow workers did their worst to humiliate him and make fun of him.

One said, "Surely you don't believe that Jesus turned water into wine."

"I don't know," the man answered. "I don't know whether He turned water into wine when He was here among us; but I *do* know that in my own house He turned beer and liquor into food and furniture!"

A young man told his father and mother that he was leaving home. He said, "I can't stand mother's piety and father's strictness any longer."

Early before daylight the next morning, the father heard the son's footsteps on the stairs and he met him and said, "Son, your mother and I haven't slept any tonight. We've been talking it over, and we have decided that there must be something wrong with us to make you want to leave home. I have come to ask your forgiveness."

The boy broke into tears. "Dad," he said, "It's not you and Mother; it's me!"

Some of the most profound truths have been given to us in the form of legends.

For example, there is the story of King Midas and the golden touch. When the king had been given the ability to see everything he touched turn to gold, he seemed to have reached the height of happiness.

Yet the golden touch turned out to be a curse for him, for everything he touched turned to gold—his followers, his food, and even his daughter.

The world, for him, became nothing more than a golden tomb.

It was suggested to a certain very famous man that his biography should be written while he was still alive.

He absolutely refused to give permission. His reason for refusal was: "I have seen so many men fall on the last lap."

It is easy to wreck a fine, noble life by some act of foolishness. It is easy to have a fine record spoiled at the last by moral failure or a cowardly act.

But St. Paul confidently tells us that he had finished his race victoriously,

About 3 o'clock one morning a Protestant pastor was awakened by the telephone.

On the other end of the line was a teen-age girl of his congregation. She said, "I'm spending the night with two friends of mine. One girl is Jewish and the other is Roman Catholic. It seems that each of these girls knows exactly what she believes. Tell, me, pastor, what do I believe?'

Well, it isn't that simple, is it? It is relatively easy to believe a little bit of good news, like your rich uncle's dying and leaving you $10,000. But it takes a lifetime of fellowship with God and studying His Word to know what we believe.

Bishop Gerald Kennedy has a bit of satire in what he says concerning Jesus' use of parables:

"If a modern preacher should tell a story with a gangster as the hero and a priest as the rascal, the congregation might wonder at his sanity."

In the parable of the Pharisee and the publican we note that one man's prayer should never have been prayed anywhere; the other's needed to be offered, and it could have been prayed anywhere.

Obviously what one does in church does not necessarily make a man religious.

Martin Martens tells a parable that goes like this:

There was once a man, a satirist. In the natural course of time his friends killed him.

People came and all stood around his corpse. One said, "He treated the whole round world as his football, and he kept kicking it."

The dead man opened one eye. He said, "But he kicked it always towards the goal!"

It required strong nerves to live the Christian life in Philippi. It was like living on the edge of a volcano.

In our personal relationships it is a great thing to have nothing but happy memories, and that was how Paul was with the Christians in Philippi.

Paul says to the Philippians: "Just as the Roman colonists never forget that they belong to Rome, you must never forget that you are citizens of heaven; and your conduct must match your citizenship."

One of the strangest stories ever to come from the mind of Henry James is called "The Beast in the Jungle."

It's about a man who waited all his life for a great moment to come. As the story progresses it soon comes to a climax of bitter tragedy when the man awakens to the discovery that the moment came and went, and he never knew it until it was too late.

We read this story and we find it to be a warning to us of the ways in which life can be wasted.

I call it "The Man Who Waited Too Long." John Marcher spent all his days waiting for that moment, and he missed life's supreme experience because he never loved unselfishly.

Rarely does a great moment of glory come when we sit and do nothing but wait.

A number of years ago Dr. S. Parkes Cadman heard a group of fine young people singing heartily the then popular song, "O, to be Nothing, Nothing!"

He thought to himself, "If they're not careful their prayer might be answered."

A missionary said that we have no right to send missionaries to foreign lands to preach a gospel which may cause commotion, divide homes, bring ostracism, suffering and even death, if we are not willing to pay a corresponding price over here.

Over there it means giving up idols, and we have no right to hold onto ours. If an idol is something we love more than we love God, we must get rid of our idol.

People who pass the Rothschild mansion in the fashionable section of London often notice that the end of one of the cornices is unfinished. Sometimes a person asks why.

The explanation is a very simple, yet suggestive one. Lord Rothschild was an Orthodox Jew. Every pious Jew's house, tradition says, must have some part unfinished, to bear testimony to others that the occupant, like Abraham, is only a pilgrim and a stranger upon the earth. The incomplete part of his house seems to say to all who pass by, "This is not Rothschild's home; he is traveling to eternity!"

Before his conversion, St. Francis of Assissi was a dissolute, self-seeking, pleasure-loving fellow. But he had no real point in living; there was no purpose in his life.

Then one day, for the first time, he came to recognize his need of God and began to understand the eternal purposes of God for all mankind. He embraced Christianity with his whole heart. From that time forward he was a changed man.

Because of the new life of Christ in him, he was able to make a greater impression for righteousness and godliness than any other man in his generation. His aimless wanderings were over when he surrendered himself to Jesus Christ.

St. Francis had the joy of God. All who read the story of the Christian centuries love St. Francis.

Why? It is his joyfulness that grips the reader. His joy sang its way in beggars' clothes around Italy, earning for him the name, "God's Troubadour." This joy of his leaped like fire to a thousand others until tens of thousands had been kindled at its torch, and a dead church, feeling that the winter was past, and the time of the singing of birds had come, awakened from its sleep in sudden resurrection—the joy, which at the last went down into the valley of the shadow of death singing.

Brother Lawrence was a lame soldier who became a monk. All his life thereafter he was only a cook in a Carmelite monastery many years ago.

He said, "I renounced for the love of God everything that

was not He; and I began to live as if there was none but He and I in the world."

We need to believe in miracles—the kind of miracle that made Simon, the vacillating, into Peter, the Rock; that made Saul, the persecutor, into Paul, the mighty apostle; that made Augustine, the pleasure-seeker, into Augustine, the saint and follower of Jesus—the kind of miracle that has taken countless human deserts and made orange groves grow in them.

Christians can face death without fear because Jesus Christ is alive!
A Moslem woman said to a missionary, "What did you do to my daughter?" The 16-year-old girl had died a few days before.
Thinking the mother was accusing him of doing something to bring about the girl's death, the missionary said: "Why, we didn't do anything to her!"
"Yes, you did!" replied the mother. "She died smiling, and our people don't die like that!"
John Wesley said, "Our people die well."

Bishop Gerald Kennedy tells about an impressive group of doctors discussing something, and then they all left hurriedly.
Somebody asked one of them where they were going, and one doctor answered solemnly that they were off to see a man who had died the day before in order to learn what should have been done to prevent his death.
We serve One who is not the God of the dead, but of the living. And we are messengers of life. But sometimes we miss our opportunities because we do not see them until it is too late.

A Spartan king boasted to a visiting monarch about the walls of Sparta.

The visitor looked around him, but could see no walls. He said to the king, "Where are those walls which you boast so much about?"

The Spartan king pointed to his bodyguard of picked troops and to another company of soldiers close by.

"These," he said, "are the walls of Sparta, and every man of them is a brick!"

Walking through the beautiful Obispado, a fine residential section of Monterrey, Mexico, I saw gardens of lovely roses. Their color, shape, and fragrance made a pleasing sensation for me, one who likes roses as well as or better than the next person.

It was January. I said to myself, "Roses in January!" What a fine thought. Even in the midst of darkness and trouble there is always a little bit of beauty if we could only see it

Look for the roses rather than the gloomy and sad things.

An Oriental king who was very unhappy summoned a philosopher to ask his advice about how to be happy.

The philosopher told him to seek out the most contented man in his realm and then to wear his shirt for a while.

But when, after a long search, they found the man. As you may have surmised, HE HAD NO SHIRT!

The Danish philosopher Soren Kierkegaard told the story of a flock of geese heading south to escape the blast of wintry winds.

The first night they landed in a farmer's yard and filled themselves with corn.

The next morning they flew on. All, that is, except one. "This corn is good," said that goose, "so I'll stay and enjoy it another day."

The next morning he decided to wait still another day. Then he stayed another day enjoying the delicious food. Soon he developed a habit.

"Tomorrow I will fly south," he said. He stretched his wings and waddled across the barnyard, picking up speed as he went. But he had waited too long. He was too fat to fly.

Bishop Hazen G. Warner tells of a young couple who went out as missionaries to India. They had worked only a few years when the husband became ill. As the days passed it became apparent that he could not recover.

His devoted wife could not accept the thought of his death. She could not make sense of it; she couldn't accept it as the will of God. In her heart she felt only rebellion and bitter grief.

She begged God for some sort of peace, some answer to the problem. None came, until one day her husband called her to his bedside and said, "My dear, you know we came here to teach these people how to live as Christians. Now we have an opportunity to show them how we Christians face trouble."

In her book *Grand Hotel*, Vicki Baum compares life to a revolving door, and one of her characters says, "The real thing is always going on somewhere else.

"When you're young, you think it will come later. Later on, you think it was earlier. When you are here, you think it is there; but when you get there, you find that life has doubled back and is waiting for you in the very place you ran away from."

A medical student in Scotland was troubled about religion. He came to his pastor in Edinburgh and said that the whole thing about religion was unreal to him.

The pastor asked, "Have you tried prayer?"

His answer was, "No, for how can I pray when I'm not sure if there is any God to pray to?"

The pastor suggested that if he actually and honestly felt that he could not pray, could not talk to a God whose existence he doubted, he give God a chance to talk to him.

"Instead of saying a prayer in the morning and evening," the pastor said, "kneel down, not saying anything, but wait quietly and see if God will reveal Himself in a very real way."

The young man went away and tried it. Some weeks later he came back to see the pastor. It had worked. He found God and God found him.

In a New York City park a crowd of men and boys, two policemen, and two employees of the Health Department gathered around a shabby, homeless tramp. He had been sleeping on a park bench and had eaten very little for several days. He was dirty and unkempt.

The policemen asked the men from the Health Department to take the man to the hospital. Those men, in turn, insisted that the man was not sick, so the police should take him to jail.

Suppose a wealthy man should come and pick the tramp up and take him to a lovely home, give him a bath and a change of clothing, and set him down to a nice table spread with fine food. He might even invite the man to listen to good music and elevating conversation, expecting him to be happy. The real change, however, would have to come from within the man.

An old preacher tells the story of a lifeguard at the beach.

A man out in the surf was apparently drowning. He was struggling and seemed to go down for the last time. The lifeguard jumped in and brought the man's apparently lifeless body to shore then brought the man back to consciousness.

A bystander asked the lifeguard why he waited so long to rescue the fellow.

"If I had approached this man while he was struggling," the guard replied, "he might have drowned both of us. I had to wait until he quit trying to save himself before I could save him."

Muretus, a Christian scholar of the sixteenth century, fell very ill while on a journey far from home.

Doctors were called to treat him as best they could with their limited knowledge of the day.

They didn't know him, and he actually looked like a waif or a tramp. So they said, "Let's try an experiment on this fellow, for he doesn't seem to be of much importance."

From the shadow of the bed came the voice of the patient: "Call not any man cheap for whom Christ died!"

The Congressional Medal of Honor was given to a young officer who, when the battle seemed hopeless, waged what his superior officers called a "one-man war." He took matters into his own hand and did the fighting of a hundred men.

When asked how he did it, he said, "I just got real mad!"

There was a great moment once in the Roman Senate when Rome had been humbled on the battlefield by the might of Carthage.

Pessimistic voices were advising surrender. "It is the only thing for us to do," they said; "we've fought and we've been beaten. Now let's compromise."

"Stop!" cried an old senator, leaping to his feet. "Remember this—Rome does not go to battle. Rome goes to war!" And the tide turned for Rome.

In the fight with your temptation, Christ's men do not go to battle; they go to war.

Sadhu Sundar Singh is remembered as one of the greatest Christians of this century. While visiting England, he was a guest of an aristocratic family, which made elaborate preparations for his welfare.

The cook went to the village grocery store to order provisions for the household. He told of the preparations being made for their guest. Those preparations included re-arranging furniture, cleaning all the rooms, putting out flowers, and planning delicious menus. He said scornfully, "You would think that Jesus Christ Himself was coming as our guest!"

A few days after the guest had gone, the cook returned to buy more supplies. The shop keeper asked with a sneer, "Well, did Jesus Christ come?"

A far-off look came into the eyes of the cook. "Yes," he whispered, "He did!"

A Christian automobile dealer in Memphis had gone with his wife, daughter, and a maid to enjoy the Great Smoky Mountains in East Tennessee. But it rained all the time. They couldn't enjoy it there, so they started home.

They spent the night in Knoxville. As they drove along the Interstate between Cooksville and Nashville, they saw a man, his wife, and two teenage children walking in the rain.

The driver stopped and said, "You don't need to walk in this rain. Get in."

The stranger replied, "No, thank you; we're as wet as we'll get. We would just get your car all wet. We don't have much farther to go, just about a mile and a half.

"Last night our house burned and we lost everything we had. We're going to a relative's house a short piece down the way."

The driver said, "I'm really sorry this happened to you. Here, let me give you something." He handed the man ten dollars.

As they drove on, the wife turned to him and said, "You weren't really sorry, or you could have given them more."

He stopped the car, took off his hat and put it on the seat between them. He had a little over $200. He put it in the hat, and said, "How much do you have, dear?" She had about $200.

"Put it in the hat!" To the daughter, he said, "How much do you have?"

She said, "I have $152 that I've been saving for this trip, but I couldn't spend any, and you've been paying for everything."

"Put it in the hat!" he said.

He asked the maid how much she had. "I'll reimburse you when we get home."

She had over $70.

He said, "Put it in the hat!"

He turned around and went back. There the people were, walking in the rain. They stopped. The driver opened the door, a hat full of money in his hand.

"Give me that ten dollars!" He said.

They gave up the ten dollars and received a hat full of money in its place.

That's the way God rewards us.

Dwight L. Moody had a friend who lost three of his five children by scarlet fever. Seeking something to cheer them, the grief-stricken parents traveled to England, to France and The Alps, and finally to Cyprus and Palestine.

One day they stopped at the bank of a stream and watched a shepherd trying to get his flock across the water. But the frightened sheep would not respond. Instead they stood shivering on the bank.

Finally the shepherd took two little lambs in his arms and, stepping into the stream, crossed to the other side. Immediately the older sheep plunged in after him, and within a few minutes the entire flock was safely on the other side, ready to find fresh, green pastures.

That was a comforting lesson for the bereaved father and mother. They no longer rebelled and complained. They realized that the Great Shepherd had taken their three children across the stream of death into the happiness of heaven, so that in God's good time the parents could follow them into God's blessed homeland.

Dr. Robert G. Lee told the following story.
In 1830 a man named George Wilson, in Pennsylvania, was sentenced to die for robbing the mails and for murder.

President Andrew Jackson took an interest in his case and decided to pardon the man. But Wilson refused the pardon and insisted to all that it was not really a pardon unless he accepted it, and he would not accept the President's pardon.

This was a point of law never raised in our country. The Attorney General said the law was silent on that point. The President was urged to call upon the Supreme Court for a decision in the matter since the sheriff needed to know whether to hang Wilson or not.

Chief Justice John Marshall, one of the ablest lawyers, gave the following decision: "A pardon is a paper, the value of which depends upon its acceptance by the person implicated. It is hardly to be supposed that one under sentence of death would refuse to accept a pardon, but if it is refused it is no pardon."

So George Wilson was hanged. Who was responsible for his death? No one but himself. The law said he must die. The President stepped between him and the law, but the man refused the pardon.

A few years ago, in a New York hotel, a maid found the body of a young man with a bullet hole through his head. On the dresser was his last will and testament, written on hotel stationary:

"I leave to society a bad example. I leave to my friends the memory of a misspent life. I leave to my father and mother all the sorrow they can bear in their old age. I leave to my wife a broken heart and to my children the memory of a drunkard and a suicide.

"I leave to God a lost soul who has insulted His mercy."

In an episode from Homer's *Odyssey* we are told of Odysseus and his weary Greek veterans of the Trojan War on their way homeward.

When they stop at a certain island they are tempted by a desire to abandon their journey because they have set foot on the land of the lotus-eaters, who eat a flowering food. These people gave the men of Ulysses a taste of the lotus, and all who ate of the honey-sweet fruit had no more desire to go home or to send tidings home to loved ones.

They were content to stay on the island, forgetful of everything else. They had been lulled into a kind of stupor, content only to exist for the moment.

Tennyson tells about it in his poem, "The Lotus Eaters." It brought lethargy and stupor and insensibility to those who ate of it.

Here is a picture that should disturb anyone who never thinks of reading the Bible and never feels any hunger pains for spiritual light or the moral guidance of God.

It is the picture of a native on the Island of Borneo or a man from Swaziland, whose ancestors were savages or headhunters. He is bowed over some pieces of paper in the dim light of a candle, laboring over a strange language in order to learn to read.

Why? There is only one reason—that he might read the Bible. He looks at this Book with hunger in his eyes, as one would look at the most priceless treasure he could long for.

He has *heard* it read, but how passionately he longs to read it for himself, to hold the Book in his own hands when he wants to, and to let it speak to him directly!

During World War I a French soldier was seriously wounded. His arm was so badly smashed that it had to be amputated. He was such a fine young man that the surgeon was grieved that the lad would have to go through life maimed.

So he waited by the patient's bedside to give him the bad news after he regained consciousness. When the lad's eyes opened, the surgeon said to him, "I'm sorry to have to tell you that you have lost your arm."

"Sir," said the young man, "I didn't lose it; I gave it—for France!"

Bishop Werner tells of a man who was found dead in a rambling New York house. He was a victim of his own plan to catch a thief or robber who might some day break into his house.

He was an odd little fellow who had little to do with his neighbors, a recluse. Nobody ever saw him or knew how he lived.

One day he tripped over a wire he had strung in a hallway in his house to trip a would-be burglar. That let fall a mountain of junk.

He was found smothered to death under a pile of old newspapers, clothing boxes, and broken flower pots.

Have you ever heard of the famous statue of Buddha in Bangkok? This ten-foot high, eight-ton statue stood in the courtyard outside a chapel for many years. People would throw trash on it and children would play on it. According to legend, it had been floated down the river from the North hundreds of years before.

In 1955 the priests decided to renovate the chapel. When it was finished, they planned to put the old statue of Buddha inside the new temple. "After all," they said, "It's a pity to leave it out there under a small tin roof with the rain dripping around the edge of it, leaving water and mud puddles around its base."

So they brought in a crane to move this giant concrete Buddha. But when this monstrous statue was lifted two feet off the ground, the ropes and chains broke, and the Buddha crashed, causing a huge crack from the shoulder to the trunk of the body.

Soon it began to rain. Darkness fell. They decided to finish the job later. They thought perhaps the priest could patch up the crack.

The next morning when the priest examined the crack in the concrete, he discovered what seemed to be a flash of gold. He began to chip at the concrete; then he saw a breastplate of gold. Soon he had all the concrete veneer off, and there was exposed the world's largest chunk of solid gold, a five and one-half ton solid gold Buddha.

This gold statue was begun in 1295 by the king of Siam. When the army from Burma was threatening to move in, the people in that little village, fearful that the golden Buddha would be stolen, covered it with cement in order to hide it. They were all killed, wiped out by the invaders, and nobody knew the secret that inside this concrete shell was this golden Buddha. Somehow it had been brought to Bangkok on a raft.

There was an hour—a grim, gray, terrible hour—when Napolean in Russia, found Moscow burning before him and his supplies fast running out.

He was forced to face westward and begin a long retreat to Paris.

He summoned the man he could best count on, the brave, gallant Marshall Ney.

"I appoint you, my Marshall," he said, "to command the read guard. You are to keep the Russians back from the main body of my troops. You are to be the breakwater between us and the deluge. You are to block their advance at any price until I can extricate my men from this trap of death and get them home safely to France."

Marshall Ney accepted the assignment. He got his troops into line and they took on themselves the full force of the pursuing

Russians, enduring indescribable affliction from wounds and frost and famine. But the French army was able to get away.

It is said that one day long afterwards when some officers were relaxing in their quarters in Paris, the door of their room opened, and they saw a disheveled figure, old and bent and emaciated, his clothing tattered, his hands trembling, and lines of suffering on his face.

"Who are you?" the officers asked. But to one of them there came a flash of recognition. "Why, it's the Marshall!" he said. All the officers rose and saluted.

"Tell us, Marshall," they said, when they had overcome their astonishment, "tell us—for we have been wondering—where is the rear guard?"

The bent, broken man squared his shoulders and looked them in the face.

"Men," he said, "I am the rear guard!" He alone had survived.

Two Indians (men of India) killed an English official in Punjab. Mahatma Ghandi was asked to save the lives of the two young men who had been condemned to die for the murder.

Ghandi refused. "I cannot condone the killing of anyone," he said.

The friends of the condemned men were furious. Some of them came rushing into Gandhi's room to kill him since he was not patriotic enough to intercede to save his fellow Indians.

As these men stood over him, Gandhi looked at them unafraid. "You may take my life if you wish," he said quietly. "It is all I have left. I have no property. All I have for you is love. If I led our people to violence to avenge this political murder, I would be using the very methods of force which I deplore. Kill me if you like, but I must stick to my truth."

It was Gandhi who said, "I would rather be torn to pieces than to disown my brothers of the suppressed classes."

O. Henry tells the story of a little girl whose mother was dead. Her father would come home from work and sit down, take off his jacket, open his paper, light his pipe, and put his feet up on a hassock to enjoy himself.

His little girl would come in and ask him to play with her for a little while, for she was lonesome.

He would always tell her that he was too tired and that she should let him be at peace. He would tell her to go out on the street and play. She played on the streets. Then the inevitable happened—she took to the streets.

Years passed and the girl died. Then O. Henry's vision extended to heaven. The girl's soul arrived at the Pearly Gates. St. Peter saw her and said to Jesus, "Master, here's a bad one on earth. Should we send her straight to hell?'

"No," said Jesus gently. "Let her in!" And then His eyes grew very stern. "Let her in, but look for a man who refused to play with his little girl, and who sent her out into the streets, and SEND HIM TO HELL!"

CHAPTER 7

Thoughts on Prayer

Prayer is the greatest power in this world. It's a pity we don't make greater use of it.

To realize that God is only a prayer away is one of the most important discoveries we can make.

Spiritual power will always vary in direct proportion to spiritual dedication.

Everything depends upon whether in prayer we are trying to *change* God's will or to *find* God's will; to make use of God or to let Him use us.

Prayer is never ours to alter or change God's will, but to ascertain it.

Many a prayer is answered, but we're often too dull to recognize the answer when it comes.

Some people look upon prayer only as a last resort to get help when everything else has failed.

When we pray we are ushered into the Throne Room for an audience with the King of the universe for an indefinite length of time.

If we are going to receive from God, we must be willing to accept what He has to give and to receive it on His terms, not ours.

Without faith, we can expect nothing from God. There is nothing mysterious about faith. It underlies all of life.

We need faith to carry us on when the church service is over and we are face to face with the daily grind of making a living

We need faith to hold us steady when we walk through deep valleys and dark days, when discouragement dogs our footsteps and we are tempted to give up the struggle, when perfection doesn't seem so perfect, and the divine is clouded by the human.

Faith is knowing that God is there even though you can't see Him, even when you can't sense His presence or feel close to Him.

Faith has come to be identified with a nebulous something or other which everyone needs when in trouble and no one needs when not in trouble.

Prayer is a force that works. It is no slot machine where we drop in a quarter and pull the lever and hit the jackpot.

Prayer is possible for anyone.

Prayer is not asking God to do something that we are not at least trying to do for ourselves. What makes our prayer real is our bringing what we cannot do in ourselves to God and asking His help.

Anyone can express himself as to what he really deeply wants. But prayer that gets results is not so much concerned with what we want as with what God wants.

If ever, since the morning stars sang together, the prayer of faith has gone unanswered or a saint has risen from his knees empty handed and defeated, then the integrity of God's government is broken, the pledges of His throne are void, and heaven is bankrupt before a claim it cannot meet.

With faith in your heart you have a series of blank checks signed by Almighty God: "According to your faith, so be it unto thee."

Until the Infinite is forced to suspend payment because His treasure house is empty, this word will not be shaken.

One of the greatest gifts of God to man is the capacity to pray. Then why is it that for all our talk about prayer, so many of us don't make it a part of our everyday living? There are some explanations, of course.

1. We live such crowded lives today that some things have to be left out.
2. We have so much confidence in our human ingenuity that prayer is not so necessary as people once thought. For example, we have the doctor, with his knowledge and wonder-drug prescriptions.
3. Some of us have had some bad experiences with prayer. We have prayed and prayed and nothing happened, so, gradually we gave up praying.

Notice the order of the Lord's Prayer. Before anything is asked for ourselves, God and His glory and the reverence due Him come first. Then other things take their proper place.

"That brief, grand prayer," as Thomas Carlisle called it, is only 70 words long, but grand beyond any speech other than its own. Here is one prayer in which every Christian can engage. It is the most private, the most public, and the most universal of all prayers.

Alas, we use it more as an incantation, than as an invocation. Short, simple, yet profound, it is as high as the sky, as wide as the world, and equal to all our mortal needs and our immortal longings.

Thomas Howard says that the real pain of suffering is not the present hurt because martyrs have proved that even that can be endured. The real pain is that God seems to have His eyes shut and His ears stopped up.

The Scriptures record scores of outstanding instances in which God has remarkably intervened at the prayerful request of His children.

In His omnipotence—by which all stars are but dust, all space but a bubble, all oceans a tiny drop, all time but a moment, and all men as grass—it is most certainly true that our Eternal God, with whom all things are possible, can marshal all His legions of angels and His own omnipotence into the answering of every true prayer of His own dear children.

Prayer is practicing the presence of God. It is the best kind of communion with Him.

I do not tell God what He must do; I ask Him what He wants me to do.

If you are in harmony with Him and His Spirit, no doubt your prayer—whatever may be its object—will be in harmony with His will. But don't ask God to abdicate His throne that you may take it.

Why should you want a second best when you can have His first best? Why should you desire your own way when His way is infinitely better?

We hold our heads in our hands and cry out at last, "Thy will be done!" What else would we want to have done?

Why not, at the very beginning, say with joy and acceptance, "Thy will be done"?

My experience in praying for a person's healing is that the Lord seldom removes the illness until it has been used to drive us back to complete trust in Him.

You say, "Well, I want the lives of my dear ones spared to me."

How do you know you do? I once knew a mother and father who prayed desperately that the life of their child might be spared, and I later saw that child become a driveling idiot.

A couple prayed earnestly that their son might live. He did. Later he became a menace to society and expiated his crimes in the electric chair. His parents went to their graves broken hearted.

Hadn't you better ask God to do what will be best, both for your dear ones and for you?

God knows our needs beforehand, but prayer completes the circuit which is not complete without prayer.

For God to answer the prayer of someone who is in rebellion against Him would be to create anarchy in His own kingdom. For God to answer the prayer of a prodigal in the far country would not be a blessing to the prodigal, but rather a curse. It would only encourage him to remain where he was.

Suppose you could go into a room where Jesus was sitting. What would you do? Would you give Him a list of all the things you want, as children do at Christmas for Santa Claus? Would you ask for the explanation of a dozen problems you haven't been able to solve?

No! You would fall on your knees before Him and kiss the hem of His garment. Just being with Him would satisfy your desires.

"They that wait upon the Lord shall renew their strength . . . . They shall run and not be weary." The picture here is of an athlete in a race. What brings defeat? He simply can't stay with it.

"They shall walk and not faint." Just to walk step after step and not faint is a remarkable achievement. Passing milestones is easier when you're going home, but even then a lot of us faint.

Oswald Chambers said, "The purpose of prayer is to find the mind of God, and then to ask for it to be done in us."

The Christian knows that he can approach God, knowing all the time that God is approaching him. Under the old order this right of approach to God belonged only to the priests. At one time only the High Priest might enter the Holy of Holies. Now we have a new and living way. We can come directly to God without the help of any priest.

Many Christians seem to think that prayer is teasing God to do something you'd like to have Him do without regard to His wisdom in the matter.

To the man who says, "What's the use of praying if you can't get what you want" perhaps the best answer is "You don't know what your want, much less what you ought to have. Only God knows." Why not ask Him instead of telling Him?

Some say, "I know what I want. First, I want money. To be poor brings so many temptations. I want money that I may never know the burden of being poor."

Are you sure? Jesus said the temptations of poverty were nothing in comparison to those of riches. He said a rich man has as much chance of getting into heaven as a camel has of going through a needle's eye.

With more than an even chance that it will ruin your soul, do you still pray for money.

"At least," you say, "I want success." How do you know you do? King Solomon had success and just look what he did with it. Do you think you would do any better?

It is not the song of the conqueror, but the song of the conquered, that has made music for the ages. Almost everybody who has amounted to anything in this world has died poor, and most of them condemned by men of their time. Yet you pray for success!

"Well, at least I want health and strength." How do you know you do? Saul and Samson had both, and look what they did. Do you think you'd do any better?

Fanny Crosby said it was the loss of her sight that saved her soul. It made her a blessing to the saints across the years. Helen

Keller—deaf, mute, and blind—has said that the greatest calamity may be God's bridge to the Promised Land.

St. Paul himself wanted health and prayed in vain for it. God said to him, "My grace is sufficient for thee."

We are urged to pray for health, but before we can do that to any advantage, we ought to settle what we are going to do with our health when we get it.

When you have learned to pray, you have learned the greatest secret of the Christian life. With the world, the flesh, and the devil bringing all their forces against you, you will need all the help God and the church can give you if you are to live victoriously.

If what you desire is in harmony with the will of God,
If it is in keeping with the teachings of Jesus,
If it will harm no one else and can add to your well-being or that of another,
If you want the will of God more than anything else,
Then you have a right to ask in faith believing.

God answers prayer. Nothing can stand before the united prayers of the people of God.

This truth was made plain to all who lived in the State of Minnesota over 100 years ago. In the summer of 1876 the grasshoppers did great damage to crops. In the spring of 1877 farmers were worried, for there was every indication of another plague which might destroy the wheat crop and bring financial disaster.

The situation was so serious that Gov. John S. Pillsbury proclaimed April 26 as a day of prayer and fasting. All schools, shops, stores, and offices were closed. People were praying all over the state. What happened? The next day dawned bright and clear. The temperature soared. This was not normal April weather for Minnesota. Billions of larvae of grasshoppers appeared. Three days of unusual heat caused millions more to hatch.

But on the fourth day the temperature suddenly dropped, and that night a heavy frost covered the ground. That frost killed those crawling, creeping locusts as sure as if poison or fire had been used.

Grateful farmers never forgot that April 26. That event has gone down in the history of the State of Minnesota as the day God answered the desperate prayers of His people.

One summer day on a city street I overhead a few words I will never forget. A mother and her little son, probably five or six, were not far from me. The boy was very fretful and was pulling on his mother's arm to get her to look in the window at a nearby store that displayed toys and candy.

After a short struggle, the mother said, with a note of exasperation in her voice, "Don't you ever get tired of wanting something?"

Probably a lot of us test God's patience by wanting and wanting, when all the while God is offering to give and give.

If we could always want what God knows we ought to have and stands ready to give, wouldn't that be wonderful? I'm sure we often don't honestly know what we ought to want.

Perhaps we need to recast our prayers. We pray for health, ease, comfort, and peace. We ask God that no trials shall befall us and no temptations come our way. Shouldn't we rather pray that God's grace may be with us in all our trials? Since we're human, we're going to have our share of trouble. We can't measure God's goodness by the extent to which we escape pain.

What harvests of fruitfulness we have seen from fields plowed knee deep by trouble! These "light" afflictions which are only for a moment work out for us an "eternal weight of glory."

Phillips Brooks offers the following advice: "Do not pray for easier lives; pray to be stronger men. Do not pray for tasks equal to your powers; pray for power equal to your tasks."

The effect of prayer is not an accumulation of gifts, but the attitude of mind which says, "Not as I will, but as Thou wilt."

Nothing can be quite so wonderful as communion with God, to talk with Him as friend talks with friend. If you're talking with God, don't hang up until He talks back.

> Prayer is practicing the presence of God.
> Prayer clears the vision.
> Prayer steadies the nerves.
> Prayer sweetens the spirit.
> Prayer makes all things possible to the one whose life is hid with Christ in God.

If you're not on the mountain top, thank God that the mountain is not on top of *you*.

Dr. Paul Rees tells the story about an insurance salesman in the East who, rather early in his experience as a tither, ran into a test that was most difficult and it almost swept him off his moorings.

While he was still a student at Purdue University, he and his wife and another couple had pledged themselves to make possible the education of a young Christian in India. It was to cost each couple seventy-five dollars a year.

One day the postman delivered a notice from the Board of Missions of his denomination that the annual payment was due. Sales for him were slow in the insurance business. In fact, the night he came home and found this notice he had had a completely futile day. He just didn't have the money to meet that pledge.

Prayerfully he laid the matter before God for several days. Nothing happened. Instead, he got a letter from the other couple telling him that twins had come to bless their home, and now, since they had expected only one child, they would have to cancel their part of the payment. Enclosed in the letter was *their* notice of the seventy-five dollars due.

So it looked as if Richard Campbell would have to meet that $150 obligation at an hour when he didn't have seventy-five dollars.

That night he decided to write several of his friends who were business men outside his own city.

In a few days a letter came from Detroit. One of the friends said he had been thinking of adding to his insurance program and would like to have the necessary forms. When the application came, it was for 50 thousand dollars worth of insurance.

With a broad smile, Mr. Campbell said, "My share of the premium made it possible for me to not only pay my share of the pledge, but the other half as well, and our boy in India was taken care of!"

CHAPTER 8

Bible Lessons

"Where art thou?"
(Gen.3:9)

Originally asked of Adam, that question applies equally to us in this day of uncertainty. The landmarks have been removed, leaving many people at sea. The cause of this uncertainty is sin.

Sin always breaks down confidence in self, in God, and in others. It instills doubts, unbelief, and distress.

I. Every person needs to be in the right place.
   A. Adam was out of place because he was trying to hide from God.
   B. Saul was out of place when Samuel was ready to inaugurate him as Israel's first king.
   C. How do we know what is the right location?
      The answer depends on what kind of foundation life is built on, our consideration of the future, dangers, storms, waves, and distress.
   D. Our surroundings are not conducive to spirituality.

II. Every person in the wrong place tries to hide. For example, the burglar, thief, disobedient child.

   A. Adam and Eve tried to hide behind fig leaves. That

was a thin barrier for God to see through. What a foolish idea!
B. Saul hid behind the "stuff."

Probably most people who are lost are hiding behind the stuff: pleasures, ambitions, business, excuses, or even hypocrites.

God knows where His creatures are hiding. He knows what we're hiding from. He knows what we're trying to hide behind. He knows, but He wants us to acknowledge our location.

If we're lost it's our own fault.

We often pray that our loved ones will "find" God. But the Bible shows us a God who is seeking *us*.

The Savior of All

"A man with an unclean spirit" (Mark 5:2)

"A certain woman which had an issue of blood twelve years" (Mark 5:25)

"One of the rulers of the synagogue, Jarius . . . besought Him saying, 'My daughter lieth at the point of death' (Mark 5:22)

The fifth chapter of Mark tells the story of three seemingly hopeless cases. It is a chapter of incurables if we speak after the manner of men.

I. The first is a demon-possessed man.
   A. Not much is said about the devil.
   B. The man dwelt among the tombs.
   C. No man could bind him.
   D. Often bound with fetters and chains, he broke them like cobwebs.
   E. He wandered in the tombs and mountains crying and cutting himself in his misery.

F. He was a terror to the neighborhood: wounded, naked, ostracized, sad, lonely, suffering, possessed by the devil.

This is a photograph taken by God's camera in all its ugly detail, in all its misery, of what the devil would do with every man but for the Hand that keeps him back.

When I see a poor man in the gutter—vile, bloody, bleary-eyed, lost—

I think, but for the grace of God, I could be there.

In this case Jesus transformed in a moment the one whom no man could tame.

Jesus is Lord of the man. No man can do without Him. You drink from His fountain; you feed at His table: you walk about His world, every bit of which is marked by His cross.

No man can be at his best until he is Christ's man. It takes courage and willpower to serve Christ, but the greatest sin a man can commit is to refuse to serve Him.

II. The second case is a woman with an incurable disease.
  A. This case was as bad as could be.
  B. She had suffered for twelve years with an embarrassing, debilitating disease.
  C. Nobody could help her. She had spent all she had on doctor bills. No doubt the doctors did their best for her. If they could have found a cure, they would have made a reputation. But they failed.
  D. One moment of contact with Jesus ended her trouble.

Jesus is the woman's Savior. Before Jesus came, women were considered toys or servants of men. In many cultures their status hasn't changed. It is any wonder that more women than men accept Christianity? What a blessing Jesus has brought to their dull, drab, tormented lives!

It is sad when a woman says "No" to Christ, but when she is the cause of her children's saying "No" it is sadder still.

III. The third case is a dead child.
    A. We often say "as long as there's life, there's hope." But this girl was dead.
    B. Jesus said, "Arise." And she sat up.
    C. Jesus said, "Give her something to eat."

        He is the Savior of the child. Billy Sunday said, "If you want to beat the devil, you must fight him with a cradle instead of a crutch." The poet Wordsworth said: "Heaven lies about us in our infancy." Jesus said, "Suffer the little children to come unto me."

        What a responsibility parents have to do everything in their power to bring their children to Christ!

These three hopeless cases—humanly speaking—prove that Jesus is Lord over devils, disease, and even death.

He Went Away Sorrowful

> "But when the young man heard that saying, he went away sorrowful for he had great possessions" (Matt. 19:22).

When who heard what saying?

To a rich young man, Jesus said, "If thou wilt be perfect, go and sell that thou hast, and give to the poor, and thou shalt have treasure in heaven: and come and follow me" (v.21).

What can we learn from his experience?

I. He was a rich man. Riches make it easy for a man to go wrong. The Bible says, "Set not thine heart upon them." You cannot serve God and mammon.

II. He came to Jesus. It is a step in the right direction. The Holy Spirit prompts us to come. Many have never done that. They have taken plenty of steps in the opposite direction.
III. He came in his youth. Most people who come to Jesus today come in their youth. Comparatively speaking, few are saved in adulthood.
IV. He came running. He was an enthusiastic seeker. Walking was not fast enough for him. Riches and morality were not enough for him. He knew he lacked something which only Jesus could provide and he was in a hurry to find it.
V. He was humble. When he got to Jesus, he knelt. He prayed.
VI. He opened his heart to Jesus. "I want eternal life, what must I do?"

He thought he could *do* something good to merit salvation.
VII. Jesus led him step by step. First He tried him by the law. "All these things have I kept from my youth up," came the reply. "What do I lack?"

Then Jesus touched the most sensitive nerve, his pocketbook. "Sell that thou hast and give to the poor." Jesus didn't say give everything to the poor, but His words doused the young man's enthusiasm. He went away sorrowful.
VIII. Where did he go?
   A. Did he go back to his riches? His riches did not satisfy and never could. Riches are convenient, but they will never get one through the portals of glory. When he left Jesus he left the riches of the skies, the treasures that never fade.
   B. Did he go back to his friends? Who could take the place of Jesus? His friends were as bad off as he was. True friends of this world are few and far between. False friends stick by you while the sun shines. They

      applaud while your purse is full. But when trouble comes, they don't know you. Jesus is a friend that "sticketh closer than a brother."
- C. Did he go back to his pleasures? Worldly pleasures provide a certain amount of gratification, but it doesn't last. Moses chose to suffer with God's people rather than to enjoy the pleasures of Egypt "for a season."
- D. Did he go to heaven? Not unless he came back to Jesus later and accepted Him as Lord. Otherwise, he sealed his destiny when he "went away sorrowful."

If you could climb the golden stairs, get through the pearly gates, look across the landscape of eternal beauty, and search through the many mansions, you could not find him. And, if you went to Jesus and said, "Where is that young ruler?" I think Jesus would say, "He went away sorrowful."

Is it possible for a man to talk with Jesus, to look into His face, and yet to go away? This young man did

Can you live with Jesus and not know Him? Judas did.

Can you die in His presence and never know Him? One thief did. In fact, he cursed Jesus in his dying moments.

If the rich young ruler, with his wealth, influence, and capabilities, had come into the kingdom, he could have been a great power for God.

Repent Ye

> "Jesus came into Galilee, preaching . . . saying,
> 'Repent Ye'
> (Mark 1:14)

The Bible, especially the New Testament, is the handbook on repentance. It commands. It urges. It enforces. It repeats. It mentions the words *repent* and *repentance* more than 60 times.

Speaking of the fate of the Galileans, Jesus said, " . . . except ye repent, ye shall all likewise perish" (Luke 13:3).

John the Baptist preached repentance. When he saw the Pharisees and Sadducees coming to his baptism, he called them a bunch of snakes. He refused to baptize them until they brought forth fruits indicative of repentance (Matt. 3:7-8). Preaching on repentance cost John his freedom and finally his head.

Without repentance, however, there is no salvation. If your repentance is shallow, your religious life will be shallow.

I. What repentance is not
   A. It is not conviction. Speak to almost anyone about Christ, and he will say, "I know what I should do." The Holy Spirit is faithful to fulfill His assignment. He leaves no stone unturned to "convince the world of sin, of righteousness, and of judgment." But it is one thing to be convicted; it is another thing to repent.
   B. It is not sorrow. Sorrow for sin is one element. You can be sorry for sin, however, without repentance. Sometimes you are simply sorry you were caught. Every criminal is sorry for his sin.
   There is such a thing as sentimental sorrow. It weeps at funerals, sad stories, or even sermons. Multitudes think they are not far from Christ because tears come easily. But it does no good to cover God's altar with tears while your heart rebels against Him.
   C. It is not promising to do better. You can promise until your hair is gray and not repent. Too many people promise only to fail. It is not enough to promise to do better.
II. What repentance is
   A. In the fifteenth chapter of Luke, Jesus gives us a beautiful picture of three cases: the lost coin, the lost sheep, and the lost son. The coin was lost through carelessness; the sheep, through stupidity; the son, through his own fault. The coin was found.

>   The sheep was brought back. The son came back of his own free will.
>
>   Repentance is being sorry enough to quit sin. It means forsaking the "far country" and returning to Christ.
>
> B. Repentance is so beautiful that it makes the angels rejoice. Jesus said, "I say unto you, that likewise joy shall be in heaven over one sinner that repenteth, more than over ninety and nine just persons, which need no repentance" (v.7).

Whatever your standing in life—rich, educated, even religious—if you refuse to repent, you will be lost.

Sin: The Telltale

> "And when the woman saw that the tree was good for food, and that it was pleasant to the eyes, and a tree to be desired to make one wise, she took of the fruit thereof, and did eat, and gave also unto her husband with her; and he did eat" (Gen. 3:16).

Sin is a voluntary violation of a known law of God by a morally responsible person. By Adam and Eve's deliberate violation of the explicit command of God, "Thou shalt not eat," sin destroyed the close relationship between God and man and brought a curse on mankind.

Infidels may croak. Theosophists may tell us we are gods. And Christian Science may argue there is nothing wrong but a derangement of the mental apparatus. But reading this account and looking at history and today's society convinces any logical thinker that sin is a reality.

One day Adam and Eve were happy, enjoying their relationship with God. The next day they were miserable. One day they were innocent. The next day they were guilty. One day life was a bed of roses. The next day it was a pit of despair with goblins crouching in the shadow. Sin cost the guilty pair both their innocence and their paradise. God drove them from the Garden of Eden.

History proves that sin is unchanging in its essential nature. What it did yesterday it will do today and it will continue to do till time rolls on into eternity.

Alexander the Great conquered the world; sin conquered him. Napoleon Bonaparte failed to conquer sin; sin proved to be his ruin. So goes the story throughout history.

We tend to treat sin lightly. No one labels it with a skull and cross-bones. But it is as devastating today as it has always been.

I. Sin leaves a sense of pollution. Only one with a seared conscience can sin and feel guiltless. If we could live life over, we might have a different story. We might cry with the poet:

> "Backward, turn backward,
> O time, in thy flight;
> Make me a child again,
> Just for tonight."
> Oh to feel the happiness of innocence!

II. Sin transforms the innocent person. Only God can bring relief from guilt.
III. Sin is hereditary. The Psalmist David said, "I was born in iniquity and in sin did my mother conceive me" (Psa.51:5).
IV. The wages of sin is death. Death to joy, peace, happiness, character, body, and brain. Eternal death to the soul.

The Soul Winner

"And they that be wise shall shine as the brightness of the firmament; and they that turn many to righteousness as the stars forever and forever" (Dan.12:3).

Compared to this promise everything the world can offer fades into insignificance. Herein lies an opportunity for the Christian to build for himself a monument more enduring than the Pyramids, more beautiful than the Temple of Solomon, and more satisfying than all the accumulated pleasures the world can produce.

The greatest task that God has ever assigned to man is that of winning souls. The command is so definite that no Christian can ignore it. The rewards are so great that our enthusiasm should never wane.

The most definite, the most concise, the most practical, and the most illuminating treatise on the subject of soul willing is found in Act 8:26-40.

In this story of the Ethopian eunuch we find every qualification for leading men to Christ.

I. The soul winner must be clear in his own experience.
   A. Philip was one of the seven men spoken of as being "full of the Holy Ghost and wisdom."
   B. Today churches have endless organizations, committees within committees, program chasing program, together with institutes and inspirational meetings ad infinitum. Philip had none of the above.
II. The soul winner must be under the direction of the Spirit.
   The angel of the Lord said, "Arise, and go toward the south." Then "Go near, join thyself to the chariot."
   Philip did not know the need of the Ethiopian. If Philip had gone his way, he doubtless would have never gone to the dreary desert with its blistering heat and blowing sand. He would probably have remained in the city with its large crowds and apparently great opportunities. But he was sensitive to divine guidance.

Sometimes God leads His children into the unlovely. For example, Livingston, Booth, and Grenfell.

III. The soul winner must be obedient.

"He arose and went" (v. 27). If Philip had been like some of us, he might have said, "I feel like I ought to go to Gaza today, but it is such a busy time for me, perhaps I'll wait till next week or send someone else." But if Philip had not been obedient, the eunuch would have gone back home with a different story.

IV. The soul winner must be an enthusiast.

"Philip *ran* thither to him" (v.30). There is something attractive about a person who is on fire for God, who has zeal for souls. Consider the four men at Capernaum who brought the sick man to Jesus. That quartet literally raised the roof.

V. The soul winner should have a tactful approach.

Dr. John Matthews once said, "For more than a half century I have been studying the easy access to the human heart." Philip did not discuss externals. Nor did he ask the eunuch what he thought about fundamentalism, modernism, pre—or post-millennialism, evolution, or other controversial subjects.

It is hard to sit on a rail fence alongside some old mountaineer and borrow his knife to whittle a stick and listen to him talk about his family, his farm, and his other interests until he will listen to you talk about your Lord. But sometimes it must be done.

VI. The soul winner should know the Scriptures.

Philip began at the Scripture which the eunuch was reading in the book of Isaiah. He explained that the risen Lord, his Master, was the fulfillment of that prophecy. Through the Word, he brought the man to Christ.

VII. The soul winner's constant theme is Jesus. Philip "preached unto Him Jesus" (Acts 8:35).

That is the message our world needs.

CHAPTER 9

Chuckles

In our language skating on thin ice can get you into hot water.

"You can do a lot of observing by just watching"—Yogi Berra

Rule no.1: Don't sweat the small stuff.
Rule no.2: Everything is small stuff.

God sometimes has to put us on our backs to make us look up.

Some day there will be a book about a middle-aged man with a good job, a beautiful wife, and two lovely children who still manages to be happy. But nobody will read it.

A businessman was questioned about his feelings toward a competitor up the street.
"There's nothing I wouldn't do for him," he said, "and there's nothing he wouldn't do for me. So we go through life doing nothing for each other."

Don't spend all your energy trying to love your enemies. Treat your friends better too.

Anyone who doesn't worry about the world situation these days must be getting lousy reception on his TV.

The best things in life are free. It's the worst things that are so expensive.

Her cooking is like Russian roulette. You never know which meal is going to get you.

By the time a man can afford to lose a golf ball, he can't hit that far.

Don't try to make your guests feel at home. If they wanted to feel at home, they would have stayed there.

When a man displays strength of character in his own home, it's called stubbornness.

Science says that success is relative. The more success, the more relatives.

I'm boss in this house, and I have my wife's permission to say so.

My wife and I are one, and she's the one.

A man showed up for work with both ears bandaged. Asked what happened, he explained:
"I was watching the ball game on TV and my wife was ironing. She left for a minute and the phone rang. I grabbed for it and put the hot iron to my ear instead."
"But what happened to the other ear?"
"Wouldn't you know? No sooner had I hung up, than the guy called again."

G.K. Chesterton, whose principles constantly got him into hot water, said, "I like getting into hot water. It keeps you clean."

A diplomat is a man who always remembers a woman's birthday but never remembers her age.

I spent a year in that town one Sunday.

Has life become a struggle between keeping your weight down and your spirits up?

There must be some sort of intelligent life in outer space. You don't see them spending billions to land on *us*.

No, poverty is not a disgrace, but that's about all I can say in its favor.

I never have trouble meeting expenses. I meet them every day.

What do we care about expenses, we have lots of them.

An insurance agent, writing a policy for an Ozark farmer asked if he'd had any accidents.
"Nope," replied the farmer. Then he allowed that a horse kicked in a couple of his ribs, a bull broke his leg slamming him against the side of a barn, and a copperhead bit him twice.
"Well," the agent asked, "Don't you call these accidents?"
"No, sir, I don't," the farmer said. "They done it on purpose."

Dr. Bradley told old Sam Barnes he should take a hot bath before retiring.
"But, Doc," Sam said, "I won't be retiring for another five years."

Why is it at school reunions you find that your classmates have gotten so stout and so bald they hardly recognize you?"

A car salesman was trying to sell an Ozark farmer a new truck. "You've got a nice place here, and with what you have you should be driving a new pickup truck when you go into town, not that old jalopy of yours!"

"I don't need a new truck," the farmer said. "Besides, I'd rather spend the money on a good cow."

"Now," the salesman responded, "wouldn't you look silly riding into town on a cow?"

"Maybe I would," the farmer admitted, "but not nearly as foolish as I'd look trying to milk that truck."

My wife is like a little girl when we go window shopping on Saturdays. So I thought it best to take her on Sunday.

Every year it takes less time to fly across the ocean and more time to drive to work.

The best way to move mountains is to begin with mole hills and work up.

What this country needs is some family trees that will produce more lumber and fewer nuts.

We never know how level headed a man can be until he begins to lose his hair.

Some pessimists complain about the noise even when opportunity knocks.

You can sow enough wild oats in 15 minutes to reap an abundant harvest for 50 years.

Money is a universal provider for everything but happiness.

Too many of us keep looking forward to the "good old days."

We used to wait until the price came down before buying something. Now we buy before the price goes up.

There are some things money can't buy, including what it used to.

It's nice to have the highest living standard in the world. Too bad we can't afford it.

Live as though every day was your last—and some day you will be right.

Americans spend $7 billion a year on games of chance and that doesn't include weddings, starting up in business, and holding elections.

A man was called before his king for some offense and was sentenced to die.
The man said to the king, "Sire, if you will spare my life for one year, I'll teach your favorite horse to fly!"
That was too good an offer for the king to turn down, so he postponed the execution for a year.
On the way out of the palace the man's wife said to him—in that tone wives sometimes use—"Why did you make such a ridiculous promise? You know you can't do that!"
"Well," the man answered. "Anything can happen in a year. The king might die; I might die; the horse might die! And, who knows, maybe I *can* teach that horse to fly!"

It's the man who waits for his ship to come in who's always missing the boat.

The best substitute for experience is being 16 years old.

I heard about a boy who murdered his mother and father, then threw himself on the mercy of the court because he was an orphan.

Today's mighty oak is just yesterday's little nut which stood its ground.

When I ask people if they are happy and they say they are, I suggest that they notify their faces.

Once upon a time a certain king built a new castle and surrounded it with a moat that was wide and deep. For additional security he had the moat filled with alligators.

Not sure that these deterrents were enough, the king devised a plan to test his moat's security. He announced that at a certain time on a certain day, the first man to swim the moat would be given a choice: He could be captain of the guard, receive a million dollars, or be given the king's daughter in marriage.

On that day everything was ready. The trumpets sounded and one young man plunged in. To the amazement of all, he swam across the moat. The king congratulated him for accepting the challenge and performing such a courageous deed. Then the king asked which reward he wanted.

"What I really want," the young man replied, "is the name of the one who pushed me!"

Fixed income—that's the income left after the car is fixed, the TV is fixed, the plumbing is fixed, and your teeth are fixed.

If your spirits are low, do something. If you have been doing something, do something different.

It's funny that being *in* hot water means trouble, when being *out* of it is the most miserable thing that can happen to you when you're in the shower.

A budget helps you pay as you go—if you don't go anywhere.

There's one thing to be said for inviting trouble; it generally accepts.

When you get something for nothing, you just haven't been billed for it yet.

It's a myth that brides blush. Actually, their faces are flushed with victory.

The perfect graduation gift for an 18-year-old girl used to be a compact. It still is—but it has four wheels.

Inflation: When you earn $5 an hour and your wife spends $6 a minute in the supermarket.

It's tough to buy a Father's Day present for a man who doesn't smoke or drink, play golf, or care how he smells.

The person who brags about how smart he is wouldn't if he were.

A man seldom makes the same mistake twice; usually it's three times more.

Anyone who is plugged in to current affairs is bound to be shocked.

What the average woman wants is a great big strong man who can be wrapped around her little finger.

The most difficult thing for a mother to remember is that other people have perfect children too.

Some day the liberated woman will discover that her most important job, the one with the greatest rewards, was right under her nose, and she blew it!

When I pass a church
I stop in for a visit.
So that when I'm carried in
The Lord won't ask, "Who is it?"

A skeptic is a person who sees the handwriting on the wall but claims it's a forgery.

A philosopher doesn't care which side of his bread is buttered; he knows he eats both sides anyway.

A man doesn't live by bread alone. He needs "buttering up" once in a while.

Look out the window from the breakfast table. You see a bird after a worm, a cat after the bird, and a dog after the cat. It gives you a little better understanding of today's news.

A preacher in pioneer days was asked, "If you believe that things are foreordained, and when your time comes there's nothing you can do about it, why do you carry a gun with you to church on Sunday?"
His answer: "Well, it's like this. I carry the gun because I just might meet an Indian whose time has come."

When I get home in the evening, I enter the door backward so that if my wife is mad at me I can start running.

Bishop Fulton J. Sheen tells the following story: He said that he went to a restaurant one morning for breakfast. He was suddenly confronted by an exceedingly courteous but coldly perfunctory waitress. She placed a menu in front of him and stood stiffly awaiting his order.
"I'll take bacon and eggs and toast and coffee."
The waitress mechanically took the menu.
Then the bishop added, "And a few kind words."
She disappeared and shortly she returned with all the goodies. She placed each item on the table with great ease. Then standing quite stiffly, she said, "Sir, will there be anything else?"
With a smile on his face, the bishop asked, "What about the few kind words?"
At this point the waitress bowed her head close to his ear and whispered, "If I were you I wouldn't eat them eggs."

The automobile has replaced the horse and buggy. But it's still wise for the driver to stay on the *wagon*.

If you think *you're* confused, think about Christopher Columbus. He didn't know where he was going. When he got there he didn't know where he was. And when he got back he didn't know where he'd been.

It's incredible when you think about it how little our parents knew about child psychology yet how wonderful we turned out to be.

Did you hear about the man who was so narrow-minded that he could look through a keyhole with both eyes at once?

An executive is one who never puts off until tomorrow what he can get someone else to do today.

Want to make your old home look more attractive? Just price the new ones.

And then there was the young man who took a job-aptitude test—he was found to be suited for retirement.

Some people's idea of keeping a secret is not to tell who told them.

It's easier to follow the leader than to lead the followers.

With today's transportation there's no such thing as a distant relative.

Don't always give your wife credit; she appreciates a little cash too.

It's trying to live comfortably that makes life rough.

A hot head seldom sets the world on fire.

No wonder women live longer than men. Look how long they are girls.

Did you hear about the man who had a terrible toothache? It drove him to extraction.

America is the only country where it takes more brains to make out the income tax return than it does to make the income.

The average husband can't afford to win an argument with his wife. It costs more to get her to stop crying than what she wanted in the first place.

Many men disappear because they know they're not wanted. Others disappear because they know they are.

No wonder a woman's mind is cleaner that a man's; she changes it more often.

Talk about others and you're a gossip; talk about yourself and you're a bore.

Men say women can't be trusted too far; women say men can't be trusted too near.

For every guy who marries for money there's a gal who marries for alimony.

Some men marry poor girls to settle down; others marry rich ones to settle up.

Marriage is like a violin. After the beautiful music is over, the strings are still attached.

Marriages may be made in heaven, but a lot of the details have to be worked out on earth.

The story of some marriages could be told in a scrapbook.

Some men wonder how they could live without women. The answer is "cheaper."

The quickest way for a man to dry his wife's tears is to throw in the sponge.

Beside every successful man stand a devoted wife—and a surprised mother-in-law.

Sometimes you can't tell if a man is trying so hard to be a success to please his wife or to spite his mother-in-law.

You can depend on a fat man—he will never stoop to anything low down.

There are two reasons why women don't wear last year's clothes: They don't want to, and they can't.

One reason there are so many juvenile delinquents today is that their dads didn't burn their britches behind them.

Parents spend the first three years of a child's life trying to get him to talk, and the next sixteen trying to get him to shut up.

When it comes to giving, some people stop at nothing.

Never trust your wife's judgment; look who she married.

I have observed—to my horror—that opportunities are not lost. Someone else always grabs the ones I didn't take.

An old-timer is one who used to drop his boy off at school on the way to work. Now he has a boy who drops him off at work on the way to school.

A hat can be used in many ways. Some folk wear theirs on their heads. The beggar passes his. The politician throws his in the ring. The cowboy carries water in his. But the majority of folk just talk through theirs.

Experience is a hard teacher. She gives the *test* first, the *lessons* later.

Did you hear about the kitten that fell into a Xerox machine and became a copy cat?

Did you hear about the dog that went to a flea market and stole the show?

"I wish I had enough money to buy an elephant."
"What do you want with an elephant?"
"I don't want the elephant. I just need the money."

Don't complain about the rain. It's the only thing coming down these days.

You might describe my financial situation as fluid. I'm going down the drain.

"I understand you had an argument with your wife. How did it end up?"
"Oh, she came crawling to me on her hands and knees."
"Is that so? What did she say?"
"She said, 'Come out from under that bed and fight like a man.'"

The modern college president has three important problems: salaries for the professors, football for the alumni, and parking space for the students.

An agnostic said to a Christian, "The idea of God never enters my head. He may exist, but I don't pay any attention to Him."

The Christian replied, "Why, man, you're just like my dog. The idea of God never enters his head either. But at least he doesn't go around howling about the matter."

Two women were leaving a hospital after visiting their husbands, who were both improving.

One said, "I know there's a shortage of beds, but I told the nurse my husband was not to leave here until he's well healed."

"My dear lady," said the other, "don't you know that from this place, only the doctors leave in that condition?"

A couple of old-timers sat on a bench listening to a candidate appeal for votes.

"Who is that fellow anyhow?" one man asked.

"I don't really know," said the other. "But he sure does recommend himself highly."

There was the fellow who stayed up all night wondering where the sun went.

It finally dawned on him.

I'm most grateful for pro football; I'd hate to have those big guys on the street with nothing to do.

I used to catch my wife in my arms every night; now I catch her in my pockets every morning.

I drew a chicken once and it was so real that when I threw it in the wastebasket it laid there.

A preacher told of visiting Yellowstone National Park with a group of tourists. He strayed from the main party who were being conducted through the park by an experienced guide.

He wandered off alone to conduct a private exploration trip on his own. But he had not gone far until he came face to face with a huge grizzly bear on a narrow mountain ledge overlooking a deep chasm.

He couldn't go around the bear, and he didn't dare turn his back for fear the bear would maul him. He had heard someone say that if one looked a bear straight in the eye, the bear wouldn't become vicious.

Being unable to do anything else, he looked the bear straight in the eye for what seemed an *unbearable* length of time. Finally the bear turned and ambled off.

Then the man started running and crying for help. The park guide heard him and rushed to his aid.

Breathlessly, he told the guide of his encounter with the bear.

The guide said, "Didn't you know that you ought not to be out here alone without a guide?"

The preacher replied, "I didn't know it when I came out here, but I know it now.

A man took his 7-year-old son fishing one day. They put out the trout lines and went to the cabin. After some two hours, they went back to the river to see if they had caught anything. Sure enough there were several fish on the lines.

"I knew there would be, Daddy," said the boy.

"How did you know?" asked the father.

"Because I prayed about it," the boy answered.

They baited the hooks again and put out the line, then went back to the cabin for supper. After supper they went back to the river and there were fish on the line.

"I knew it," said the boy.

"And how?" his father asked.

"I prayed again."

They put the line back into the river and went to the cabin.

Before bedtime they returned to the river. But this time there were no fish.

"I knew there wouldn't be," said the child.

"How did you know?" asked the father.

"Because," said the boy, "we forgot to bait the hooks."